PRAISE FOR *ASK YOUR ANIMAL*

"Through stories, examples, and an array of intuitive communication exercises, Marta Williams leads readers into the wonders of animal communication and the benefits of living in the present moment. Marta's attention to all aspects of creation, including wildlife and creatures in our backyards, makes attunement to the inner world of animals possible for anyone who is willing to take this incredible journey with her."

— Allen and Linda Anderson, authors of
Angel Animals: Divine Messengers of Miracles

"I highly recommend this book. Marta's books have been very valuable in my own development in communicating with horses and other animals, but *Ask Your Animal* is my favorite. It touched my heart profoundly and has inspired me to go even deeper into my own relationship with horses."

— Carolyn Resnick, natural horse trainer and author of
Naked Liberty: Memoirs of My Childhood

PRAISE FOR *LEARNING THEIR LANGUAGE*

"Marta's delightful book is an inspiration, and it demonstrates clearly why, and how, anyone can communicate with animals . . . a must-have for any animal lover."

— *Natural Horse* magazine

"Animals have senses that transcend our five, and it is within this realm that true communication with all life occurs. This wonderful book by Marta serves as verification of and instruction in the magical world of animal communication."

— Marty Goldstein, DVM, holistic veterinarian and author of
The Nature of Animal Healing

"In our society's blinding addiction to reason, our intuition has nearly been extinguished. Allow the message in this book to rekindle your inner connection with all life."

— Julia Butterfly Hill, activist and author of
The Legacy of Luna and *One Makes the Difference*

PRAISE FOR *BEYOND WORDS*

"Marta Williams does it again! Her moving and profound message of the vital and everyday nature of interspecies communication is crucial to helping us remember our place in the natural world."

— Derrick Jensen, author of *Language Older Than Words*

"This is a book with a pulse, the heart of which is in its compassion for animals. Marta Williams not only talks with the animals but teaches her readers to do it too. This book offers exquisite moments of attention, much needed."

— Linda Hogan, author of
Dwellings: A Spiritual History of the Natural World and *Power*

"My dog Jessie and I were fortunate to be able to attend a workshop with Marta Williams. I feel anyone who lives with and loves animals will benefit from her insight and her innate ability to teach."

— Catherine Ryan Hyde, author of
Pay It Forward and *Electric God*

"Marta Williams is a luminous guide and teacher. Her book beautifully shows how you can learn and practice this art and skill for yourself."

— SARK, author and artist of *Make Your Creative Dreams REAL*

ASK Your Animal

Resolving Behavioral Issues through Intuitive Communication

Marta Williams

Foreword by Vanessa Williams

New World Library
Novato, California

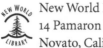 New World Library
14 Pamaron Way
Novato, California 94949

Text design by Tracy Pitts

Library of Congress Cataloging-in-Publication Data
Williams, Marta.
Ask your animal : resolving behavioral issues through intuitive communication / Marta Williams ; foreword by Vanessa Williams.
    p.   cm.
Includes bibliographical references and index.
ISBN: 978-1-57731-609-1 (pbk. : alk. paper)
1. Pets—Behavior. 2. Human-animal communication. 3. Animal communication. 4. Human-animal relationships. I. Title.
SF412.5.W56 2008
636.089'689142—dc22   2007051481

First printing, April 2008
ISBN: 978-1-57731-609-1
Printed in the United States on 50% postconsumer-waste recycled paper

New World Library is a proud member of the Green Press Initiative.

10   9   8   7   6   5   4   3   2

Contents

Foreword

I first learned of Marta Williams during a moment of sheer panic. It was Memorial Day, May 28, 2007, at 10:45 AM. Our feisty year-old Yorkie, Enzo, appropriately named after the maker of the Ferrari, sped down our driveway chasing our car. He did this often as we drove away, always stopping at the front gate, sniffing around a bit, and then heading back up to the house. My last image of Enzo that day was of his little tan face and fluffy black body in the rearview mirror. As I caught my last glimpse of him running after us, I commented to my fourteen-year-old son, Devin, "Look how cute Enzo is." The convertible top was down. It was a gorgeous, sunny day as we headed four streets away to drop Devin off to meet the middle school band to march in the town parade.

I returned in less than seven minutes and was surprised to see a large SUV stopped on a private road. I had passed it on the way out but grew concerned now to see it stopped at the foot of my hill. As I waited for the Expedition to move, it pulled over to the side of the road so I could drive by. When I pulled into my driveway and closed my front gate, I assumed Enzo was inside the house. Once inside, I called to the rest of the family to get ready for the parade because it started at 11:00 and we wanted to get good seats. My eldest daughter, Melanie, decided to stay home and lounge by the pool since it was such a beautiful day.

The rest of us left the house and headed into town, thinking that Enzo was poolside with Melanie. We watched Devin march by playing his sax, waved to our neighbor Hillary Clinton, and remembered our veterans in a ceremony at the Chappaqua Train Station. We drove home, opened the door, and were surprised that Enzo wasn't there to greet us as he always is. I went upstairs and then out to the pool to ask Melanie, "Where's Enzo?" She said she didn't know, probably somewhere in the house. That's when I knew something was horribly wrong.

Enzo

The image of that dark blue Expedition stopped on my road ...the gut feeling I'd had to close my gate immediately...it all made sense now. After calling for Enzo and searching every wooded path and pond, I knew I had to call the police to report a stolen animal.

The Mt. Pleasant police came quickly, and I gave my report to a very sympathetic officer who was also a fellow pet lover. I described the vehicle I'd seen loitering about, but I didn't have a license plate number.

The officer told me that since Enzo was a small-breed dog, a coyote or a hawk could have gotten him. I politely listened but knew in my heart that coyotes and hawks don't drive dark blue Expeditions and that Enzo was a smart and speedy dog. My next step was to call the local cable station, Channel 12, who had a crew over to the house in minutes. I wanted to get the message out that Enzo had been taken, provide a photo, and ask that he be returned to a veterinarian's office or shelter.

Then we got to work. The whole family, my assistant, and Kathi, my nanny of seventeen years, made posters to spread the word that Enzo had been taken. I prayed that he would be well treated and stay alive. After getting only two phone calls claiming an Enzo sighting — which didn't pan out — by Thursday, May 31st, I had Brian, my assistant in Los Angeles, make an appointment with a pet psychic. He didn't think I was crazy. We both knew the police didn't have any leads and the posters weren't leading anywhere. Too many days had gone by, and I was close to tears each time I walked past Enzo's empty dog bowl. We searched on the Internet and started making phone calls.

The first psychic we called said Enzo was alone near a whitish-gray or tan building. She mentioned a lot of rockery, an old gate or gazebo, and a grassy area near a garage. "He's trying to escape but can't," she told us. "Sit on the ground, take a deep breath, and bring a squeaky toy." Rockery, arched gate, gazebo? That was our front yard and our neighbors' yard across the street! We ran down with Enzo's squeaky toy and sat on the ground and beckoned him to come. Part of me was so desperate to find any sign of him. He may have been injured or caught in a trap. That night we called his name and searched with flashlights. Then the rain started to fall. Still no response. We prayed to St. Anthony of Padua, the Saint of All Things Lost, and we amped it up with the Miraculous Responsory of St. Anthony, returning together to pray as a family each morning and night.

My assistant searched for other pet psychics in hopes of getting new leads. I kept coming across Marta Williams's name on the Internet and had Brian arrange my first phone appointment for Friday, June 1st, at 10:00 AM. Marta asked me to describe Enzo's personality and said she would call me back in an hour, after she communicated with him.

When Marta called back, the first thing she said was that Enzo had told her, "I'm a good boy. I would go home. I wouldn't run away." I almost burst into tears at that moment because I knew he was a good boy and would never wander off our property. She confirmed he had indeed been picked up by a man and a woman and offered a treat (possibly chicken) and driven about thirty or forty miles southwest in a dark blue SUV. She even gave me the SUV's license plate number to give the police. She felt that he was being held in a cage with other dogs around and that the food was bad. The building was away from other buildings. Marta sensed that Enzo's captors could be part of a ring that sold breed dogs like Yorkies.

Enzo had a microchip that contained all my contact information, and by this time I had already alerted Home Again (the pet microchip company) that Enzo was missing. Marta said to search Pet Hunters, to continue with the flyers south of our community, and to check black-market websites.

She told me to call her the following day, after she checked in with Enzo again. On the second reading, Marta had looked at a map of our area and brought up Yonkers as a place of interest that was thirty miles southwest. She suggested that we travel down the highway, go to the second exit under the overpass, and continue straight to the water. All this was Enzo's vision of where he had traveled days before. A fish market came into Marta's head as well as airplane hangars or a structure that looked like hangars in the water. She thought it possible that the people who took Enzo knew he was my dog and were keeping him as part of a bigger group of dogs all housed in a big white building near an overpass. Well, that was all I had to hear. Enzo was alive being held captive in a cage, hating his food and the people who took him. I called Kathi, my nanny, and grabbed my flyers and a baseball bat, and was ready to go get my dog. Kathi drove, and since we were traveling to uncharted neighborhoods, she brought a crowbar in the back seat.

As we traveled thirty miles south on the Saw Mill Parkway toward Yonkers, I had my bat in hand and read Marta's instructions. We exited heading toward the Hudson River, went over the train tracks, and found hangars right next to the water. They didn't have airplanes in them but instead housed a taxi repair service. We turned around, searching over the overpass, and saw a white building that looked like a small warehouse some

distance from the others. I
immediately took photos of
the building and tried to go in
because I saw stacks of dog
food through the window.
But where was the fish
market? We drove the area,
writing down license plate
numbers of any dark Expeditions, but we found no fish
market. I just knew Enzo was
in that building. We circled
around the block and entered
the street from the other di-

*Vanessa (far right)
with her kids and dogs*

rection. There, at the corner of the road, stood a restaurant with
a big fish in the window. Bingo! I knew this was the right place.

On my third reading with Marta, I told her how immensely
accurate she had been with the area. She told me she had consulted with other colleagues to help with more information. She
felt Enzo was still in the same place. Two men and a woman with
a white truck in front of the building were near him. Marta asked
one of her colleagues to help on the case. This person had a different perspective. She, too, felt Enzo had been taken, but she did
not think he was as far south as Yonkers.

She told us we would hear something on the eighth day of
Enzo's disappearance. Another colleague of Marta's felt that Enzo
had been taken out of New York to a New England state. The captors knew the heat was on because in every TV interview, I mentioned that Enzo was stolen and that he was microchipped with all
my information. I never knew how many animal lovers there were
in the media!

On June 5th, eight days since Enzo had disappeared, I got a
call from Davis Animal Hospital in Stamford, Connecticut. The
vet on the phone asked if I was Vanessa Williams, and I said yes.
Then she said, "We have your dog." I asked if she was sure, and she

said she had swiped the chip and that's how she got my number. The vet told me that the person who brought Enzo in said she knew me. I asked her to put the other woman on the phone. She did, and the woman said she had worked as a nanny for a friend of mine in town. Then she told me her mother had found Enzo wandering the roads in a neighboring town miles away. Not my good boy — sounded shady to me. I got off the phone, ran to tell the family, and loaded up the kids in the car to go to Connecticut. Since I was being given an award in Manhattan that night, Kathi drove the kids to pick up our miracle dog. When she got there, Enzo's fur had been completely cut, he had a new collar, and the woman said he hadn't eaten. Bingo!

I called the police and told them Enzo had been returned in another state, and they were gobsmacked! They immediately came to the house to officially interview me again for a possible dog-napping case. I told them the same story I had given them eight days before. Now they knew I wasn't crazy! The police interviewed the woman who allegedly found Enzo in the next town over, and guess what her daughter drove into the station's parking lot? A dark blue Expedition with New York plates!

The story they told started to get shadier and shadier. The son was the one driving the SUV on Memorial Day, and the daughter gave a different reason for returning Enzo in Connecticut. I decided not to press charges because I was so happy to have Enzo back.

Marta sent me on a journey that uncovered a building with a suspected illegal dog ring, told us a time frame, gave us tools to work with, and kept hope alive. And we had a great ending!

This experience taught me that intuitive communication is useful for all animal lovers in good times and bad. I know you will find many practical ways to help your animal by reading this book. And I think you will love all the stories in it. I hope you never have to find a lost animal, but if you do, it will be nice to know you can turn to *Ask Your Animal* for guidance.

— Vanessa Williams, actress and singer

Acknowledgments

My cat Hazel used to curl up in a basket beside the computer whenever I wrote, helping me with ideas and inspiration for my first two books. Just as I started *Ask Your Animal,* Hazel died from kidney failure at age twenty-four. As you might imagine, I was devastated. Without my cat coauthor at my side, it was hard to want to sit down and write. My once-feral cat Tule came to my rescue. She stretched out in the basket and gave me a look with her sea-green eyes that said, "What are you waiting for? Let's get going." She made it possible for me to keep writing even through the loss. For that I am blessed and grateful. I offer what I believe to be good advice throughout this book, which I have collected from friends and mentors over the years, a few of whom I would like to specially thank. For all things horsey, my thanks to Tiffany Ashcraft and Kelly Michalec, and for their infinite dog and cat wisdom, my thanks to Christie Keith and Lisa Pesch, DVM. I am fairly certain that this book will teach and entertain you simultaneously and seamlessly, not because of my skill as a writer, but because of the stories. Thanks to all the animals and humans who contributed to this book. Your wonderful stories deserve to be read around the world. A special thanks to Vanessa Williams for writing the foreword and sharing how connecting intuitively with her lost dog Enzo helped secure his safe return home.

This book wouldn't have happened if New World Library hadn't seen its potential. I am grateful for the opportunity to get this information out to people. Good editors can make a book great, and I had some of the best: Georgia Hughes, editorial director at New World Library; my sister, Susan Williams; and copy editor, Jeff Campbell. I appreciate all their meticulous work. A new book means another chance to work with my favorite publicist, Monique Muhlenkamp. My thanks to text designer, Tracy Pitts, for a lovely interior, and to cover designer, Mary Ann Casler, for being so cheerful and professional during what turned out to be an extensive search for the perfect cover.

Introduction

A little brindle-colored Plott hound showed up on my porch recently. He was starving and so malnourished that he was half the size of a normal adult Plott hound. He had old bite marks all over his body from being attacked by dogs. He cowered when I went to pat him on the head, which is a sure sign that a dog has been beaten. He wanted to be rescued. He gets on well with my dogs, so I decided to keep him if he can fit in with my other animals, and if not, I will find him a good home.

The very first thing I did was to have a long talk with him, out loud. I spoke with him as if he could understand every word I said, explaining exactly how he would need to act with the horses and the cats if he hopes to stay here. After our talk, I closed my eyes and imagined him doing exactly what I had asked. To test him out with the horses I walked him down to the barn. He started to run after them, but he stopped and sat immediately when I informed him, "You have to be nice to the horses and leave them alone." As we walked among the horses I told him, "You need to stay away from their feet and be calm around them all the time." Within minutes he got it and was expertly moving around the horses like he'd done it all his life.

So far so good, though I still have to see how he is with the cats. As long as he isn't highly aggressive, I am sure I can have the new dog and my cats tolerating each other within a week, just by telling them what I want, why I want it, and then visualizing them getting along. I will probably have to think up some bribe to entice my cats to participate in this venture. And I may have to add in some traditional, positive-reinforcement training sessions to successfully make the shift in the hound's behavior, but the process will still be faster than using just traditional training alone. I know this because I have been successfully using telepathic or mind-to-mind communication, which I call intuitive communication, for over a decade now with my animals and my clients' animals to create harmony between animals and to resolve other behavioral issues. I work as an animal communicator, assisting people with their animals and helping them hear what their animals have to say.

Like almost everyone else in the world, I started out believing that being able to communicate intuitively with animals was pure science fiction. However, I was fascinated by the idea. I sought out novels that featured telepathic connections with animals, and I loved to daydream about what it would be like if people and animals could actually connect in this manner. I must have read every book written by Marion Zimmer Bradley and Andre Norton. I remember the thrill of reading one story about a woman who could talk with her snake, which she used to help cure people of illness and injury, and another story about a woman who was a falconer and could exchange thoughts with her hawks. I had no idea, while reading those books, that people could actually do what was depicted in them, or that I would end up devoting my life to helping people all over the world recognize and develop their ability to communicate intuitively with animals and nature.

My view of the world changed forever when I went on a retreat in the White Mountains of California. It was there that I learned of a woman who reportedly taught people how to communicate intuitively with animals. I was fascinated by the prospect and hopeful that it was not just fantasy. I couldn't wait to take a class, and signed up as soon as I returned home. The results of that venture, however, were mixed. I was fairly certain that the teacher and a few of the students in the class could indeed communicate mentally with animals, but I had serious doubts about my own abilities. My background is scientific. I have a master's degree in biology, and at the time I took the class I was working as an environmental scientist. My training as a scientist made me skeptical of the invisible ability to communicate intuitively. I realized that to believe I was capable of mental communication with animals, I would need some hard evidence. So I embarked on the most interesting scientific experiments I have ever conducted.

Essentially, I ended up teaching myself how to communicate intuitively with animals. The first thing I did was read every book I could find on extrasensory perception, telepathy, psychic ability, and intuition — all of which I consider to be different words for the same thing. The most inspiring of these books was *Kinship with All Life* by J. Allen Boone. Boone, a Hollywood screenwriter in the 1940s, tells the story of how a famous TV dog, Strongheart, taught him the silent language of intuitive communication. If you could only read one book on animal communication, that would be the one to choose. Once I understood the basics of how to send and receive information mentally and emotionally, I began practicing. I talked to anything that moved and mentally greeted every animal I saw. I remember one dog in particular who had his back to me when I sent him a mental greeting. In response he whipped around, did a complete double take, and then tried to run over to greet me. His incredulous owner commented, "Wow, he really likes you for some reason." I talked to wildlife — butterflies, deer, hummingbirds, and ants. I even talked to the plants in my garden, encouraging them to grow and bloom. My friends, family, and the scientific colleagues in whom I confided thought I had gone around the bend! But I didn't care; by then I was too fascinated to do anything but continue my experiments.

Because I am a trained scientist, I made sure that at least some of my work was replicable and verifiable. I did that by asking domestic animals questions and then checking with the people who knew the animals to verify my results. Often I did this without anyone even knowing what I was doing. For example, at the vet clinic I would intuitively question a cat in the waiting room about why she was there, and then casually ask the same of her person. Or at the dog park I would ask a dog if he liked children or if he liked to swim, and then I'd ask the animal's person the same question about the dog, offering up some pretext for my interest. In this manner I evaluated whether I was accurate in what I received, and therefore able to converse intuitively with animals.

After about six months of practice, I had some breakthroughs where I received information I knew I could not have made up. That finally tipped the scales and convinced me of my ability and accuracy. Now that kind of thing happens every day for me. In a recent case, I talked at a distance with a dog I had never seen. Knowing only her name and description, I picked up from her that she was a stray who had been starving and that she really liked someone named Cheryl. The dog's owner confirmed that the dog had been a stray and was starving when picked up. She also said that Cheryl was the dog's favorite trainer.

I tell my students that they may need to have several such convincing experiences before they can accept their own ability to communicate intuitively. I think that is because we are so conditioned in modern culture to believe that intuitive communication is impossible, even more so when it is we ourselves who attempt it. After my initial success, I kept experimenting and found my accuracy slowly increasing. I started to work part-time as an animal communicator, taking on real cases. One was a horse who was acting up. The horse's owner was being encouraged to sell the horse, and she was heartbroken because she didn't want to part with him. She hoped I would have a solution. When I talked to the horse, he told me he had a rib out of place, which was why he was acting so badly. A chiropractor treated the horse and found a rib significantly out of place. After the treatment, the horse's disposition returned to normal. In another case, I helped a woman find her elderly dog, who showed me that he was stuck in a creek at the bottom of a long hill. The hill and creek the dog mentally described to me matched the terrain where the woman had been searching, but she had not gone all the way down to the creek to look for her dog. When she did that, at my suggestion, she found him.

I have had thousands of experiences like this in the course of talking with my clients' animals. I am now completely convinced that intuitive communication is real and that anyone who cares to learn can do it. The information I have collected in my experiments over the years falls into the category of anecdotal data, which is often subjective and not measurable. However, in intuitive communication with animals one is able to verify accuracy and do replicable experiments, so the data collected is scientifically significant. In fact, there is so much evidence of the accuracy of intuitive communication that what is not credible is to *deny* its significance. Yet mainstream science does deny it, perhaps because admitting that intuitive communication is real would necessitate major revisions of scientific theory and practice with respect to other life-forms. I decided long ago that I wasn't going to worry about what mainstream scientists thought or wait for them to catch up to this field. I decided to venture out to the edge of this frontier and make the ability accessible to those who wanted to learn it.

That was more than a decade ago. Now I work full-time as an animal communicator, helping people with all kinds of problems with their animals. I travel around the world to teach people how to communicate intuitively. I've found that all people have this gift; we are born with it. We've just been trained to suppress it, and we've been taught to believe that it is impossible. That is simply not true. The world does not work the way we were taught. Anyone can talk to animals and hear what they have to say. However, because of our cultural conditioning, learning how to do it can be a bit tricky. That is what I have been determined to remedy. I spent years developing techniques for teaching people how to communicate intuitively as quickly and painlessly as possible, and

I have written two other books on the subject. In *Learning Their Language*, I give detailed instructions and exercises for communicating intuitively with animals and nature, and *Beyond Words* is a collection of success stories from regular people like you who learned to communicate intuitively.

In *Ask Your Animal* I focus on helping you learn to intuitively hear your own animals and be heard by them, and I show you how to apply intuitive communication to resolve common behavioral problems you may encounter with your animal. You will also learn how to use intuitive communication to assist shelter animals and other animals in distress, find lost animals, deal with the death of an animal, and work to create harmony and balance within your home and between humans and the natural world.

The process of intuitive communication can be divided into two parts: sending and receiving. Sending is the easy part. Sometimes just talking is all you need to do to remedy a troubling situation with your animal.

My sister's friend Debby Hand adopted a husky-mix puppy who had been abandoned in her neighborhood. The dog lived in the fields and was almost feral when he was taken in and somewhat tamed by a neighbor. Debby agreed to take the dog, whom she named Sparkey, when her neighbor could no longer care for him. She soon found out that Sparkey was a biter. When she would go to grab his collar, he would

Sparkey

bite her, though not hard. Debby didn't really want to keep him, but she couldn't give him to anyone knowing he was a biter, and she was sure he would get euthanized at a shelter. My sister gave

Debby my book *Learning Their Language*, and Debby decided she had nothing to lose; she might as well try talking to Sparkey about his biting. She explained out loud to him that biting was not an option: "If you keep this up, Sparkey, you will die. You just can't keep biting." The following day, Debby grabbed Sparkey's collar without thinking. Sparkey started to bite her, but stopped himself and slowly withdrew his mouth from her hand. From that day forward, he never tried to bite Debby again. How would you explain his sudden change of behavior, unless he had heard and understood Debby? Sparkey has turned into a wonderful, loving dog who is great with kids.

MORE STORIES

Another story along these lines comes from friend and colleague Adele Leas.[1] Adele sponsors a horse named Cali and rides her every day along the banks of the Mississippi River in New Orleans. One day, she called to tell me that she had been out with Cali, walking with her and letting her graze along the river, when Cali managed to slip out of her halter. In panic, Adele realized she had a fired-up horse ready to run, with a train track on one side, a busy road on another, and a group of children approaching from yet

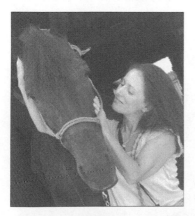

another direction. The train was just in sight coming down the track. The situation couldn't have been worse. Adele said that something took over inside her. She calmed down, and in a strong, sure voice started talking to Cali as if the horse could completely understand her the way a person would. She said to her, "Cali, you are not safe. You have to come over here to me right now." To Adele's surprise

Adele and Cali

and delight, Cali trotted right over and let her put the halter back on. Adele told me she credits my books with saving Cali's life. She said, "If I had not known about intuitive communication and not believed that Cali could understand me, I would not have given her those commands."

Sending information to animals by talking out loud, or by sending feelings or images mentally, can be learned quickly. You may have to work a bit harder at mastering the ability to receive information intuitively, but this ability can also become easy with practice.

Another example of a successful beginning attempt at intuitive communication comes from one of my students, Jeanne Joslyn. This incident occurred before she came to my classes, and it gives you a sense of how intuitive communication can be received and of how such information can be vague and hard to trust initially. My advice to beginning students is to always go with the first thing that pops into your head.

A small dog was hit by a car in front of Jeanne's house. The dog's collar had a tag with a phone number. Jeanne called the number and reached the dog's owner, who agreed to meet her at a nearby veterinary hospital. To transport the dog, Jeanne put on a makeshift muzzle and then gently lifted the dog into the back seat of her car. She sat with the dog as her husband drove them to the clinic. She felt sorry for the animal, as she was obviously in pain, and she tried to think of how to calm her down. Then she remembered seeing me on TV on *Animal Planet* suggesting that people experiment with talking to their animals by setting aside disbelief and assuming that the animals could understand every word that was said. On the show, I told people to accept whatever information popped into their heads as being potential intuitive communication coming from their animals, and Jeanne had been trying out these techniques with her own animals. She was doing it more for fun than anything else, because when it came right down to it, she really didn't believe that it was possible. Like most beginning communicators, she thought that she was making up everything that she perceived mentally.

But for lack of a better idea, she talked to the injured dog, explaining where they were going, that the dog's mom would be meeting them at the clinic, and that the doctors would help her and take away her pain. The dog looked so sweet that Jeanne decided to take off the makeshift muzzle, saying out loud, "I don't think you're going to hurt anybody." Suddenly, Jeanne heard the word "Daisy" in her head so clearly and strongly that she thought to herself, "Daisy? Where the heck did that come from?" She looked at the dog and realized the possibility that the dog might be telling her her name. Jeanne said out loud, "Is that your name? Daisy?" all the while thinking to herself that she was going to feel awfully stupid when they got to the clinic and the owner called the dog by a different name. Then Jeanne thought, "Okay, let's test this theory! Let's prove it wrong and stop this foolishness right here." She asked the dog what her owner looked like and how the dog had gotten lost. The dog sent Jeanne a mental picture of a heavy-set woman with reddish hair, along with the idea that she had gotten lost in the woods while hunting rabbits and was unable to tell which way was home.

When they pulled up at the clinic, a woman was waiting for them who was not at all like the one the dog had described. As soon as the car stopped, the woman opened Jeanne's car door and lifted the dog out, saying, "It's okay, Daisy. It'll be okay now." Jeanne was stunned. She sat in the car, unable to move as the truth washed over her. The dog really *had* told Jeanne her name. Still astounded, she pulled herself together and walked into the hospital where the woman was sitting with Daisy in her lap. Then the front door opened and a heavy-set young woman with auburn hair rushed over to Daisy. As she passed, Jeanne thought to herself, "Well, *that* woman has red hair." The woman holding Daisy looked up at Jeanne and pointed to the redhead, saying, "She's the owner. I'm just a friend of theirs."

Jeanne almost lost it. She grabbed her husband by the arm and dragged him outside. "That dog just told me her name and what her mom looked like!" she ex-claimed. Her husband looked confused, so Jeanne told him the whole story and asked if he thought she was nuts. Her husband was surprisingly sup-portive, saying there were many things that we can't explain in our world, and if Jeanne thought the dog talked to her, then he believed her. Jeanne still felt that she might be making things up. So she went back inside and asked the wo-men how Daisy had become

Jeanne with her dog

lost. "Oh," the friend replied, "her husband was out hunting with Daisy a few days ago, and Daisy didn't come back when he called for her."

YOU CAN DO THIS, TOO

Without exception, anyone is capable of doing what Jeanne did. I know because I have trained thousands of people to talk with animals and I know you can learn, too. In chapter 1, I explain what intuitive communication is and how it works, and in chapter 2, I teach you, through a series of simple exercises, how to communicate intuitively with your own animals. In chapter 3, I suggest exercises for improving your newfound skills and creating a better relationship with your animals. In chapter 4, I show you how intuitive communication skills can help create harmony between all the animals in your household. Chapter 5 focuses on using intuitive training techniques to enhance any kind of training situation you are involved in, while chapter 6 explores a variety of intuitive techniques for correcting common behavioral issues, including separation anxiety, lack of confidence, aggression, inappropriate urination, acting out, and running away.

In chapter 7, I go beyond behavioral issues and teach you how to talk with animals you don't know in a shelter or rescue situation, and how to assist an animal who has been abused or traumatized. Chapter 8 provides specific instructions for using your intuition to find lost animals, and chapter 9 deals with how to use your intuition to transform the experience of going through the death of your animal. Chapter 10 offers instruction in connecting intuitively with all of nature, including:

- Talking with wildlife in your area
- Warning wildlife of potential dangers
- Managing pests
- Helping your garden grow
- Working with medicinal herbs

Finally, in the epilogue, I discuss the impact that intuitive communication is having on our world and the promising use of a related ability — conscious intentionality, or manifesting — to help restore balance and health to the animals and the earth.

I wrote this book to make the skill of intuitive communication available to you so that you and your animals can have the best possible life together. I wanted to share the amazing stories my clients, students, colleagues, and friends have sent to me about their experiences with intuitive communication, and I have included many of these stories for you to enjoy, along with photographs of the storytellers and their animals. I hope *Ask Your Animal* will be widely read and will help humans become more respectful and compassionate toward animals and the natural world, adding to the worldwide effort that is now underway to save and restore this brilliant planet.

CHAPTER 1
About Intuitive Communication

*A*nimals are masters of intuitive communication. Unlike us, no one ever trained them to repress their intuition. They never had anyone tell them that mentally sending and receiving thoughts and emotions was silly or make-believe. Animals know that staying tuned in to their intuition helps them to optimize life and make the best choices from moment to moment. No matter how domesticated the animal, he or she is always aware that following your intuition can mean the difference between life and death. This would explain why many animals involved in the Asian tsunami in 2004 moved to higher ground right before the wave hit, while most people did not. While some people did sense the tsunami and sought higher ground just as the animals did, many others may have had some kind of internal warning, which they then disregarded.

Animals pay attention to the information that comes to them intuitively as hunches and feelings. Humans, on the other hand, have been trained to disregard such impressions as inconsequential. From the moment we are born, we are subtly, and sometimes overtly, conditioned to tune out our intuition. Intuitive information often comes in the form of feelings, and feelings are not so acceptable in our modern-day, ultralogical culture. As we grow up we are encouraged to suppress emotion and rewarded for being rational. Do you recall any of these phrases from your childhood?

"Honey, you are just imagining things."
"You know animals can't talk."
"Be grown-up."
"Don't be silly."
"Don't make things up."
"You don't know that; you can't prove it."
"That's impossible."
"Don't get emotional."
And for boys: "Stop acting like a girl."

We actually receive information from our intuition all the time — like getting a definite feeling, good or bad, about someone we have just met — but we block ourselves from recognizing it. Fortunately, we aren't completely successful at this, and our intuition regularly breaks through our barriers, especially in a crisis. Have you had any of the following intuitive experiences?

Knowing when someone is lying to you or manipulating you.
Getting a strong feeling that you should (or shouldn't) do something (and finding out you were right).
Knowing from a distance when something is wrong with your baby or one of your animals.
Thinking of someone and getting a call or letter from the person.
Knowing how someone is feeling.
Knowing something is going to happen before it does.
Knowing who is calling before you pick up the phone.

Intuitive communication is the hypersensitive ability to pick up and transmit information without speech and without relying on body language; it is sending and receiving information mentally and emotionally. Although often considered a New Age phenomenon, I view it as an ancient skill that is now being revived. I believe our ancestors were as adept at intuitive communication as animals are today, and that they were in constant intuitive connection with one another and with all aspects of nature.

With their unobstructed intuitive senses, animals are able to read minds. They know what a person or another animal is thinking and feeling and are able to see, in their mind's eye, the images in the mind of another. One of my students, Triny Fischer, told me this story about how her now-deceased dog, Nora, demonstrated this ability.

Nora was a 120-pound malamute and the incident happened several years ago when they were in Florida for the winter. Nora had always lived in cold climates, and she was finding the heat and humidity of Florida not to her liking. To lift Nora's spirits, Triny would take her to the beach at sunrise and sunset. They always went to one particular beach because it was rarely crowded and had a lovely wooded trail that ran along the shore. The beach was once a hangout for nudists, and even though nudism was illegal, it was not unusual to see a nude swimmer or sunbather there. Triny was not bothered by this and paid little attention to it.

Triny describes Nora as a wonderful, loving dog who simply adored all people. But Nora didn't like small white dogs. One particular evening at sunset, Triny noticed a woman and her small white dog following behind them on the beach. Triny tried to hustle Nora up and put some distance between them and the little white dog. As she did, she caught sight of a nude man crouched behind some bushes. When Nora saw this man, she stopped and would not move. Normally, Nora would happily approach anyone she met on the beach, nude or otherwise. Triny put Nora on a leash and

Nora

tried to make her keep walking. In response, Nora did several uncharacteristic things. She barked at the man, refused to move forward, and raised her lip when he stood up. Nora only moved when Triny started walking in the opposite direction, away from the man. This irritated Triny because she didn't want to have an unpleasant encounter with the little white dog, but Nora, being 120 pounds, got her way. The woman and the white dog circled around them and continued down the beach. As Triny and Nora headed toward the car, the man appeared out of the bushes a few more times, and each time Nora would make a low-pitched howl and walk faster. Once they reached the car, Nora was perfectly fine, as if nothing had happened.

The next morning, Nora and Triny returned to the beach and found yellow police tape everywhere. Triny learned that the night before, just after sunset, a woman walking the beach with her small white dog had been raped, beaten, thrown into the water, and left for dead. The woman had regained consciousness and dragged herself onto the beach. Her dog had alerted a couple walking on the beach, who then discovered her. The woman received critical medical care that saved her life. Triny told the police about her own experience the previous evening, and her description of the man matched the one given by the woman. Triny knew that Nora had saved her from that man. From then on she paid keen attention to any intuitive warnings Nora gave her. One could speculate that Nora had actually been reading the man's body language, not his emotions or thoughts, but Triny did not see anything unusual about the man. He was not acting in an aberrant manner, as far as she could tell.

HOW INTUITIVE COMMUNICATION WORKS

Intuitive communication is not about reading body language. You do not even have to see an animal you wish to talk with. You can just get a description of the animal, connect emotionally, and start sending feelings or thoughts to the animal mentally. Information can be sent or received mentally as an emotion, a physical feeling, a picture, a word, a phrase, an idea, a scenario (like a movie), a smell, or a taste. Sending information intuitively to animals is easy because they are so good at receiving. Learning to receive information back from animals can be more difficult, since we are so used to repressing the intuitive information we receive. Intuitive messages can take a while to sink in, as this story from another student, Karen Hudson, illustrates.

Karen sold her horse, Sundust, to someone she thought would be a good match. But it didn't work out, and the people sold the mare to someone else. They told Karen they'd found Sundust a good

Karen and Sundust

home, but a couple of years later Karen started to have dreams about Sundust, and felt she should check up on the horse. She decided to run an ad in the paper. When there was no response, she gave up. But she kept on getting the feeling she needed to check up on Sundust, so she ran another ad. Someone eventually responded, and Karen found out that Sundust had been passed to seven different people and had even been sold at auction. Karen now believes that the feelings she was having about Sundust corresponded to times when the horse was being mistreated. She is sure that Sundust was calling out to her for help using intuitive communication, but the only time Karen's busy mind could quiet down enough to hear was at night in her dreams. As it turned out, Karen was able to buy Sundust back, and she plans to keep her for the rest of her life.

I equate the ability to perceive intuitively with ESP (extrasensory perception), telepathy, your sixth sense, and psychic ability. Everyone is born hardwired with intuitive abilities; we have just forgotten how to use them. Two researchers in the field of intuitive communication, Danny K. Alford (known as Moonhawk)[1] and Walter Greist,[2] concluded that intuitive communication is the foundation underlying all spoken communication.

Based on the results of experiments he conducted, Greist hypothesized that every time we speak we are concurrently sending intuitive information. For example, if you tell someone about your wonderful vacation at the ocean, you are at the same time and without your volition or awareness sending the person images of where you went, physical feelings of how it felt to be there, and emotional feelings that you had while there. Conversely, if someone is telling you about her great hiking trip, you are receiving from her, without realizing it, images, sensations, and feelings of the experience she had while on her trip. The trick to communicating intuitively is to gain conscious control and awareness of this process, which is, as I've said, now largely unconscious in most modern human beings.

Moonhawk, who was part Native American, combined his studies of indigenous cultures, quantum physics, linguistics, and parapsychology into an integrated field that he termed "quantum linguistics." Moonhawk put forward the hypothesis that intuitive communication is the prototype of language. He identified intuitive communication as the "old language," used by all indigenous cultures, and the method for achieving communication between all forms of life on earth.

He felt that no concept of language would be complete unless it included the idea of the "old language." He saw intuitive communication as a basic flow of meaning and perception, a primitive form of knowing. He defined the ability to read the emotional intentions of another as a system of information transfer that predates the development of speech and provides the foundation of language. He claimed that without the continuing unconscious operation of the "old language" in the background of our consciousness, the words we speak would make no sense. The limitations of current models of linguistics, he stressed, are that they do not allow for consciousness or telepathy as active factors in human communication. Moonhawk, as a student of indigenous languages, felt that these languages more closely approach intuitive communication. He designated intuitive communication, not Esperanto, as the true universal language, for it is a language already possessed by all people and all species on earth.

Spoken Language Versus Intuitive Language

Intuitive communication does not have a lot in common with the linear, spoken, word-based communication we consider to be true communication. For one thing, with intuitive communication, you can convey whole stories and lifetimes of data in a nanosecond. When I intuitively ask a shelter animal to tell me about his past, I often receive an instantaneous download of information on his early life as a puppy: whom he went to, how his previous people treated him, how he felt about them, what his previous houses and people looked like, and why he ended up at the shelter.

Another difference is that you can do this from a distance; you do not have to be present with an animal to be able to talk intuitively. I know this from my own experimentation with animals over the years, and it has been the experience of every other animal communicator I know. Researcher Ronald Rose documented this same ability in Aborigines. In the 1950s, he spent seven years among Aboriginal tribes in Australia, studying and documenting their intuitive abilities.[3] Rose found that the tribespeople he studied could send and receive information intuitively over long distances. In a pretechnological culture such as that of the Aborigines, where there was no form of long-distance communication and tribes were separated by many miles, it makes sense that people would have a highly developed ability to communicate intuitively. Most often, the information the Aborigines received had to do with an illness or death of a family member, and much of the data was corroborated by witnesses outside of the tribe, such as missionaries or cattle ranchers. It is interesting that the Aborigines would sometimes receive the information by conversing with a totem animal, rather than from direct mental contact with a person.

A final difference between intuitive and verbal communication is that intuitive communication can transcend linear time. For example, one can converse with the spirit of an animal who has died and get accurate information about that animal. Lori Ammerman, another student of mine, found this out after reading my first book, *Learning Their Language*. In the book I suggest that people try to communicate intuitively with my animals, including my horse Dylan, who was alive when I wrote the book in 2003. When Lori connected with Dylan in 2007, she experienced an overwhelming feeling of sadness. Then the idea popped into her head that Dylan had died, which had in fact just occurred. There would have been no way for her to know that except through intuition. So even after an animal dies, you can still connect and get information about the animal, since in intuitive communication you are connecting with the higher self or spirit of the animal.

In chapter 2, I will teach you in detail how to communicate intuitively with animals, but the basic process is easy to describe. You send information either by speaking out loud, thinking a message, or sending a feeling or an image to the animal. Remember, animals are masters at this; rest assured that they will receive what you send. To receive information, you make contact with the animal mentally and emotionally, and then pay attention to every intuitive impression that comes into your awareness. It is best to record these impressions as you perceive them because it can be hard to track and remember them otherwise. While this process may sound easy, its simplicity is deceptive. What most people find is that their rational minds try to take over the process, striving to choose the "right" or more plausible answers, which effectively cuts off intuition. With practice you learn to override your rational mind and focus instead on the flow of information coming to you intuitively.

SCIENTIFIC RESEARCH INTO
INTUITIVE COMMUNICATION

How is intuitive communication possible? The best answers to that question come from quantum physicists. Some of the best analysis of the research in this field has been done by Lynne McTaggart.[4] In her most recent book, *The Intention Experiment,* she reviews the major researchers and experiments that have contributed to current theories about how our world works and how intuitive communication might be possible. I will summarize McTaggart's findings, but even though I had an ex–rock star for a physics teacher in college, it was never my best subject.

The theories of quantum physics are at a great divergence from the accepted theories of Newtonian physics. Quantum physicists propose that the universe is not a place where all objects move within three-dimensional space according to fixed laws of motion and time. Rather, the universe is more like a single organism of interconnected energy fields in a continuous state of becoming. This continuous interconnected energy field is called the Zero Point Field, so named because even at temperatures of absolute zero, where one would expect an absence of movement, tiny fluctuations of matter are detectable. This constant fluctuation and movement is termed entanglement. Physicists postulate that the Zero Point Field activity is affecting all particles and all matter, equally, throughout the universe. In other words, we are all connected by this field of energy — we are all one, we are all entangled.

By virtue of this constant connection and energy entanglement, we are in contact with all beings and all things in the universe at all times. Using our intention, we can focus, connect, and communicate with whomever or whatever we choose. In discussing the significance of this theory, McTaggart writes:

> If all matter in the universe was interacting with the Zero Point Field, it meant, quite simply, that all matter was interconnected and potentially entangled throughout the

cosmos through quantum waves. And if we and all of empty space are a mass of entanglement, we must be establishing invisible connections with things at a distance from ourselves. Acknowledging the existence of the Zero Point Field and entanglement offers a ready mechanism for why signals being generated by the power of thought can be picked up by someone else many miles away.[5]

Another important researcher into the existence of intuitive communication is Cleave Backster,[6] a lie-detector specialist who discovered that living organisms could read and respond to human thoughts. His work includes some of the most comprehensive experiments conducted to prove the existence of interspecies telepathy, most of which, oddly enough, were done using plants and invertebrates. Backster stumbled upon his discovery one day in 1966, when, out of curiosity, he hooked up his lie-detector equipment to his dracaena plant. A lie detector measures increases and decreases in electrical resistance. An increase in resistance in a human subject indicates stress, which is present when someone is lying. Backster watered the plant and then put the electrodes on a few leaves sandwiched together to see if there would be any change in resistance when the water reached the leaves. He expected to see an upward trend in the ink tracings, corresponding to a drop in the plant's electrical resistance as moisture increased. Instead, he saw a downward trend and a short spike, mimicking a human stress response. He assumed that he was observing an emotional response from the plant.[7] To test further, he decided to find something that would cause an immediate dramatic response in the plant. He tried putting the plant's leaf in his coffee, but got no response. He realized he would have to do something more dramatic. He thought about getting a match and burning the leaf. At the moment he had that thought, his recording pen went to the top of the strip and almost jumped off. The plant had reacted just to the thought of being burned.

Backster conducted untold numbers of experiments proving

that plants and animals are telepathic. He even showed that plants reacted when something else was harmed, such as when a group of brine shrimp was killed. He recorded evidence of a reaction to human emotional highs and lows, especially to threats or some kind of negative intention, in paramecia, mold cultures, eggs, and even yogurt. He discovered that these reactions were not dependent on distance: there could be a reaction to his thoughts whether he was present with the plants or separated by many miles. He concluded that the organisms he studied were not just reacting to his thoughts but were communicating telepathically with everything alive in their environment. He discovered, too, that plants could learn to tell whether someone really intended to do them harm or not.

Backster's work is unorthodox; because of this, he has not received the support and recognition he deserves. It took the investigations of two respected physicists, Fritz Popp and Konstantin Korotkov,[8] to finally legitimize Backster's findings. These two researchers discovered that thought transmissions are occurring constantly within organisms (from one part of the body to another), between organisms, and between an organism and its environment. The vehicles for these transmissions are quantum light emissions called biophotons. Thoughts are, therefore, equivalent to a stream of photons. As such, they can travel through time and space. It appears Backster was right: plants and animals can intercept and perceive human thoughts, and we theirs.

Few scientists dedicate themselves to the study of telepathy in animals. One of these is Rupert Sheldrake, a British microbiologist. Using statistically verifiable research techniques, he proved, with very little probability of error, that in a controlled environment with no possibility of environmental clues, animals could predict when their owners were coming home. His book *Dogs That Know When Their Owners Are Coming Home*[9] is about this and other intuitive or psychic phenomena in animals.

The bulk of evidence for intuitive communication with animals is being collected by people actually engaged in animal communication, both professionals and students. This body of information is anecdotal, and as such is largely disregarded by mainstream science. However, anecdotal evidence is the basis for many traditional scientific inquiries, such as human drug and pain studies. The sheer volume of anecdotal evidence for the existence of intuitive communication between species ought to qualify it as significant data.

A WORD ABOUT ACCURACY

Most people who do intuitive or psychic readings claim an 80 to 90 percent accuracy rate for the information they receive. In my classes, I ask students to connect intuitively with an animal and write down their impressions. Afterward, they verify these impressions with the animal's person, placing a check mark next to something that is accurate, an X when it's inaccurate, and a question mark if the answer cannot be verified. I consistently observe a high level of accuracy in my beginning students. Within the first hour of training, they are able to achieve rates of 70 to 90 percent accuracy for their testable results. After they have checked their answers, I ask students to go back and circle the impressions they feel they could not or would not have made up themselves. These are the results that end up convincing people that intuitive communication is real and accurate.

For example, Susie Henkel asked the dog she was connecting with whether he liked children. In response, she got a positive feeling. Then she saw a picture in her mind of a blond girl with a ponytail in a pink ski jacket. The dog's person corroborated this information, saying, "Oh yes, that's my niece. He loves her. He loves all children."

In one exercise, I have people ask an animal they don't know to describe his or her home, both inside and out. The results can be spectacular, with accurate and specific descriptions of vegetation, architectural design, colors, decor, flooring, and the layout of rooms — information that would be impossible to know except by intuitive communication.

This rate of accuracy is achievable with practice. There is always the chance for error or bias, so one must take that into account. What tends to happen to beginning students is that after a few successes at intuitive communication, their rational brains kick in and they start to question, critique, and doubt themselves. The process then is to find a way back to that experience of receiving easily and accurately. As I tell my students, I don't have to teach people how to communicate intuitively; they already know how. My job is to teach people how to recognize and become convinced of their ability.

EXERCISE
Reclaiming Your Intuition

To reclaim and revitalize your own intuition, the first place to start is with your emotions. Often in my consultations, I will convey what I hear from a person's animal, and the person will respond, "I knew that was true. I had a feeling about it, but I didn't trust myself to believe it." Feelings are the front lines when it comes to intuition. If you have a feeling about something, pay attention to it; don't just brush it off. Keep a diary and write down those vague musings, then reread them later to review what your intuition told you. Most of the time, what we feel turns out to be true. But we are trained to completely override this inner navigation system, following instead the advice of just about anyone but our own selves!

Intuitive information can come to you in a variety of ways: feelings, images you see in your mind's eye, memories of other situations that have relevance to the present, and words or phrases that pop into your head. Some people even get virtual sensory data, like phantom physical feelings, smells, and tastes. The key to reclaiming intuitive information is to accept it. Try this experiment: Whenever you find yourself in a quandary about a decision between two or more options, try consulting your intuition. Get a pen and paper and sit quietly. Consider each option and record your intuitive data for each. To do this, first set your intention to receive intuitive guidance about each option. Then write the first option at the top of the page. Now immediately begin sensing what intuitive data you are receiving and write it down. I liken this process to a radar scanner. Your sole purpose is to recognize incoming data and record it. Don't judge it or try to alter it; just record it as accurately as you can. Again, you may receive feelings, thoughts, memories, or other data. No matter what comes in, just write it down. Do the same for each option. Then compare what you have written. My guess is you will have received some pretty clear guidance about what to do, courtesy of your intuition.

Another technique for jump-starting your intuition is to pay close attention to how you are feeling in any given situation. Make it a habit to stop and do an internal check of your emotions. If something doesn't feel right, it probably isn't! The consequence of ignoring your feelings is that your intuition will retreat and become less and less apparent and accessible. If you want to truly hear the messages from your intuition, you have to honor your feelings.

CHAPTER 2
To Hear and Be Heard

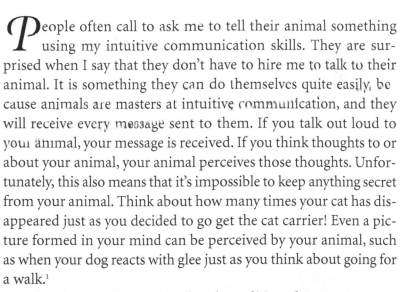

*P*eople often call to ask me to tell their animal something using my intuitive communication skills. They are surprised when I say that they don't have to hire me to talk to their animal. It is something they can do themselves quite easily, because animals are masters at intuitive communication, and they will receive every message sent to them. If you talk out loud to your animal, your message is received. If you think thoughts to or about your animal, your animal perceives those thoughts. Unfortunately, this also means that it's impossible to keep anything secret from your animal. Think about how many times your cat has disappeared just as you decided to go get the cat carrier! Even a picture formed in your mind can be perceived by your animal, such as when your dog reacts with glee just as you think about going for a walk.[1]

If we had not been trained and conditioned to suppress our intuition, we would be as good at intuitive communication as animals are. However, while you can trust that your animals hear and understand you when you talk to them, or mentally send them information, what you can't bet on is how they will react to what you say. Just because they can hear you doesn't mean they will do whatever you ask, any more than a person would.

You may be a total animal lover, like I've always been, and you talk to your animals out loud already, but chances are you don't truly comprehend how much they can understand of what you are saying. That was true for me, and it is the case for most people I know. It wasn't until I studied intuitive communication and started experimenting that it dawned on me that my animals were hearing and comprehending everything I said to them.

Author and horse trainer Carolyn Resnick[2] discovered this shortly after reading one of my books. She saw a dog locked in a car in a parking lot. The dog was not in any danger or overheated, but he was panicking — barking and racing back and forth between the front and back seats of the car. Carolyn tried talking to him intuitively. She sent him the mental thought that his person would be back soon and that he was perfectly okay. She told him he could stop barking and settle down. To her amazement he froze in midstride, looked at her, sat down, and did not move or open his mouth again.

Karen Berke, a former student who now works professionally as an animal communicator, had a similar experience one day when she was volunteering at a center that brings horses and handicapped adults and children together. Karen was taking care of a miniature horse named Buddy, grooming him and walking him through the rural neighborhood surrounding the center. On the walk, they passed several properties where dogs would race along the fence line and bark. That day there was only one barking dog: a yellow Lab. The dog raced up and down the fence line as Buddy grazed a little. The dog was going crazy. Karen had asked him to calm down in the past with no results. This time she had a longer talk with him. She said, "You are racing

Karen and Buddy

so fast you can't even bark!" All of a sudden, the dog slowed down and stopped running the whole length of the fence. Instead, he ran right in front of Karen and Buddy. Karen was amazed. Then she told him that he could relax, because she and Buddy were not interested in his property and were just there to have some grass. The dog abruptly stopped barking and running, looked right at Karen, and then turned around and walked to the back of his yard. He didn't even come back as she and Buddy were leaving.

When you start talking to your animals as if they can truly understand you, you may observe some shifts in their behaviors and attitudes. It's as if they are saying, "Well, she finally gets it! Okay, let's play this game now."

That was Kelly Boesel's experience with her horses. Kelly feeds her horses every morning on her way to work. Her horses are in a large pasture, and in the past Kelly had to hike over a hill or two to find them and bring them in for their feeding. One day Kelly decided to try an experiment. She had a talk with her horses out loud as if she were talking to a group of people. She asked them if they would be so kind as to meet her at eight every morning at the gate so she wouldn't have to go on a hike to find them. The next day, like magic, there they were, waiting for her at the gate. Now she talks to them in the car as she drives to the pasture, telling them she is on the way. They must be hearing her because they are at the gate every morning now.

I believe that all animals are sentient. Each species has its own priorities and physical abilities that affect how its intelligence is displayed. But the notion that animals are not as smart as humans is incorrect; their intelligence is just different from ours. When you start communicating intuitively with animals, you will begin to perceive the unique intelligence of each species and each individual.

Animals also experience the same emotions in the same intensity that we do. Maverick ethologist Marc Bekoff wrote a book exploring this theme, called *The Emotional Lives of Animals*.[3] Most scientists, though, have not reached the point of conceding that animals can feel as humans do. But whatever the scientists say, animal lovers know that animals have feelings that run as strong and as deep as humans. Animals show us their emotions all the time through their behavior. How else would you explain the behavior of Taffy, the horse in the following story?

A client of mine, Debbie Erdman, regularly rode her elderly horse Taffy on trails and along the beach. When Taffy turned thirty-eight, Debbie thought it might be

Debbie and Taffy (now forty-eight)

too much for her to go for long rides along the beach anymore, so the next time Debbie went she rode another horse instead. When she got back, Taffy gave her the "cold shoulder" all day long, turning her back whenever Debbie approached. Taffy made it clear that she was not happy about being excluded.

From then on, Taffy always went on trail rides. If it was a long ride, she would go on a lead rope while Debbie rode her other horse. Debbie still rides Taffy, who is now forty-eight. Taffy loves to be out in front, and she is a marvel when it comes to teaching other horses not to be afraid on the trail.

SENDING INFORMATION INTUITIVELY

Here are some exercises to help you practice sending information intuitively to your animal. As with all the exercises in this book, keep a notebook with you so you can record your results and chart your progress as you go along. Get a sturdy notebook, one that will last a while and hold up in the field.

EXERCISE
Talk as If They Understand

For the next two weeks, suspend your disbelief and act as if your animal can understand everything you say, think, or feel. Talk out loud to your animal as you would to a person. Explain everything you are doing. Tell your animal when you will be home and why your animal can't go along when you leave. Every day, explain things out loud as much as you can to your animal. By the end of two weeks, I am certain you will be convinced that your animal really can hear and comprehend you intuitively.

EXERCISE
Think, Feel, Visualize

Talking is one way to send information. In the following exercises you will also practice sending information mentally by thinking, feeling, and visualizing. You can do these exercises in the presence of your animal or at a distance. Your animal does not have to be paying attention to you when you do this. He or she can be playing or even sleeping. Your animal will receive your communication regardless. Some animals will make it apparent that they have received the information, and some won't. These are experiments; write down your results and reserve judgment for later.

Thinking

Think of some quality you admire in your animal and, in your mind, form a compliment about that quality as if you were speaking to your animal. Your thought might be something like, "I am impressed with how well you interact with other dogs." Send that thought mentally to the animal by closing your eyes and imagining the thought traveling through the air. Have the intention that the thought is sent and received.

Feeling

Think of a feeling you would like to send to your animal, perhaps a feeling of love or gratitude. Form that feeling in your heart by thinking of some time in the past when you felt love or gratitude. Now picture opening doors at your heart, and imagine the feeling traveling over the air to your animal. Have the intention that the feeling travels through the air and is received.

Visualizing

Some people do not visualize easily. If that is true for you, do the following exercise using your feelings instead. Many people who at first have told me they couldn't visualize were able to do so once they began communicating intuitively with animals.

Visualize (or feel) an image of something pleasant you would like to send to your animal. This could be an image of a fun activity you will soon be doing, or some treat you will give your animal. Imagine that image traveling over the air to your animal. Have the intention that your animal receives it.

EXERCISE
Ask for Proof

Ask your animal to do something that will prove to you that he or she is hearing you. Merlaine Agresta did this with her horse, Bump. She was standing outside Bump's stall and told him out loud how much she loved him and how important he was to her. She kissed his nose and said, "You know, I wish you would kiss me, just once, to show me how much you love me!" With that, he turned to her and licked her face. This was not his usual behavior, and Merlaine was stunned to learn that she and Bump could talk.

HEARING ANIMAL MESSAGES

Animals are always trying to get through to us. They are constantly sending us intuitive messages that we aren't aware of. However, in spite of ourselves, some of those messages are getting through. When you think your dog might need some water, and you check and find the bowl is empty, chances are that your dog sent you that message intuitively. You just didn't register it that way. When you get good at intuitive communication, you will be able to hear what your animal wants and needs. Animals are thrilled that we are finally learning to hear them. It makes their lives so much easier.

In the absence of direct intuitive communication, animals have to resort to other means to communicate and get us to understand. Pamela Ginger Flood told me this story about her horse Midnight when he was trying to give her an important message.

Pamela was moving and had to trailer Midnight and her other two horses to her new home. Midnight hates trailers. When the trailer came to pick up the horses, they loaded the youngest horse, Mikey, first, because he was so easygoing. Then they were going to load Midnight and, finally, Pal, the older horse. It took twenty minutes to load Midnight. He just stood there at the end of the trailer. Sometimes he would look like he was about to get on, but then he would glance in at Mikey and stop. Finally Midnight loaded. As soon as Midnight walked toward the back of the trailer, Mikey body-slammed Midnight and came unglued. Pamela and her friend were in danger of being slammed into walls and trampled. Midnight deliberately used his body to block Mikey from hurting them, all the while keeping an absolutely calm demeanor. He stood there like an immovable object, while Mikey tried to back over him. Midnight did not flinch or move an inch. Mikey eventually calmed down, and the women were able to load Pal.

Midnight had known there was danger, but Pamela was too task-oriented to hear him telling her that Mikey was not safe. Pamela said that was the third time Midnight had saved her from serious harm, which proves another one of my axioms about animals: they are altruistic, even though most mainstream scientists insist they aren't.

Pamela with Pal and Midnight

Receiving is much harder than sending because we have been conditioned to resist the process. In school, we are taught to be critical thinkers, and critical thinking is death to intuition; the more schooling we've had, sometimes the harder it is to learn to receive messages. Simply put, to receive intuitively, you connect with the animal, scan for impressions, take the first things that come in, and accept what you get without judgment. It sounds easy, and for a few lucky people who didn't get a lot of social imprinting, it is. For the rest of us, there are some blackberry patches to cut through.

Modes of Intuitive Reception

Before you try your hand at receiving, it helps to know what an incoming intuitive impression can look like. There are six ways you can receive information intuitively: knowing, seeing, hearing, feeling, smelling, and tasting. Here is a description of each of these modes of receiving.

Knowing

Intuitive impressions often occur as a sense of knowing that comes to you quickly. You will just know something is true, but you won't have any idea how you know it. The term for this mode is called "clear knowing," or claircognizance. I well remember the day I asked my black Lab Daisy if she wanted me to have her put to sleep. She sent me the sure knowledge that she was ready to go.

Seeing

This mode of receiving is more easily experienced if you close your eyes. You may become aware of pictures or scenes like a movie that come into your mind. Once, a horse I was communicating with showed me a clear picture of a little gray kitty. I saw the kitty standing in the stall next to the horse. I knew this image came from the horse because it was not something I would have thought of. When I asked the horse's person about it, she told me the image was accurate and that the kitty and the horse were inseparable. This form of receiving is called "clear seeing," or clairvoyance.

Hearing

You can receive words and phrases, or whole sentences and paragraphs, mentally. At first this will sound and feel like you are talking to yourself, although some people hear different tones of voice and accents from each animal they talk with. A lost cat I was talking to once told me he was "up high." I had his people searching all the trees in the area; it turned out he was on the neighbor's roof. This mode is called "clear hearing," or clairaudience.

Feeling

Feelings can come intuitively in the form of emotions or as physical feelings. You can intuitively sense how an animal feels about something, and you can sense when an animal is not feeling well physically. In one of my cases, I communicated with a horse who was very contrite and worried about his bad behavior, which he said he couldn't help because his teeth were so painful. An equine dentist checked his teeth and discovered major problems. Once these were corrected, the horse behaved much better. This mode is called "clear feeling," or clairsentience.

Smelling and Tasting

Receiving impressions in the form of virtual smells or tastes is less common than the other modes, but one can still receive this way sometimes. When I work with lost animals, I make a point of asking them what they are smelling and tasting, because that can give clues as to their whereabouts. In one case, a cat sent me the smell of Chinese food, and it turned out he had accidentally been locked in the basement of the Chinese restaurant next door to his house. Receiving a smell intuitively is called "clear smelling," or clairallience. Receiving a taste intuitively is called "clear tasting," or clairambiance.

Which Mode Should You Use?

There is no right way to receive intuitively. You may find when you try the exercises in this chapter that you receive most easily in one or two specific modes, such as feeling and pictures. Everyone is different; what's easiest for you may be more difficult for others. After much practice I can receive in all of the above modes. Moreover, when I ask the animal to send me information in a particular way, I can get it. The bottom line is that it doesn't matter how you get something, as long as you get something.

Opening to Intuitive Impressions

When you open up to receiving intuitively, you become the human equivalent of a radar scanner, searching for incoming data in your field of awareness and recording it. Your goal is to record this information exactly as it comes to you, avoiding the temptation to change it to make it seem more sensible and acceptable. Try to keep what you record pure and true to what you perceive. Don't presift, qualify, judge, or reject any incoming impressions. Your job is to recognize and record. Record everything, even if it seems obvious, silly, made-up, stupid, or strange. If nothing is coming in, make your best guess — that will help prime your intuition and get you going.

The approach I just described took me a long time to figure out, and it is key to receiving easily and accurately. If you can follow that guidance, you will have a much easier time.

Enlisting the Aid of Your Inner Critic

At first, when you communicate intuitively, you will feel like you are making things up. This will be especially true when you talk with your own animals. That's because you know so much about them that it will be hard to be objective. Your logical mind may take over and inhibit you. Some people are very hard on themselves and become completely discouraged about their ability to communicate. To counteract this, make a deal with your inner critic. Decide on a time frame for your experiment in intuitive communication — three months would be good. Then ask your inner critic to help you capture data and record it during that time, rather than judging and dismissing what you receive. At the end of three months, you can review your progress and decide if you want to keep experimenting.

The Need for Proof

It is important for your logical mind to be able to see proof that intuitive communication is real. In fact, that is the most important thing to establish. Once you learn how to talk with your own animals, I will teach you how to talk to animals you don't know and to ask questions that can be verified afterward. The results from such verifiable experiments can be overwhelmingly convincing, as you will see in the following story.

Following one of my classes, Kendra Wilson, like many brave students, took my advice on how to practice and began talking intuitively to everything that moved. This is really the best way to practice, as it gets you talking all the time. Her friend was skeptical of her abilities until Kendra had a conversation with a mule that turned out to be amazingly accurate.

They met the mule at a draft horse driving and cart show.

Kendra saw two mules, a brown one and a white one, tied up and went over to say hello. The brown mule had on a light horse sheet that said, "Champion Coon Jumper 2005." Coon jumping is a sport only mules can do that involves jumping straight up from a standstill over a bar; it's similar to a high jump but without the running start.

Kendra was talking to the brown mule and congratulating him for being a champion when the white mule started hee-hawing. He pushed the brown mule out of the way and put his face right up to Kendra. She intuitively heard the white mule say, "No, I'm the champion. I'm the champion. It's me! It's me, not him!" She said to the white mule out loud, "Okay, calm down. Okay. You are the champion. Are you happy now?" The mule did seem to calm down at that point. Kendra explained to her friend what had happened, and they decided to test out the results by going to the coon jumping contest that was to be held in a few hours. If both mules competed, Kendra and her friend would see for themselves who was the better jumper.

As they walked away, the white mule started to make a huge fuss again. Kendra turned back and asked him intuitively what was wrong. He told her that he wanted her to come back and scratch his ears. She complied, and then they left again. This time he was quiet.

When the contest was announced, Kendra and her friend could hardly believe it when the white mule appeared dressed in a rhinestone halter and a fancy sheet with rhinestone borders bearing the title "Coon Jumping Champion 2008, White Lightning." Kendra waved to the mule and called out, "Hello, Lightning!" The mule looked right at Kendra and began hee-hawing loudly. Kendra and her friend realized at that point that they had had a private audience with not one but two coon jumping champions.

Signs of Intuitive Communication

When you get intuitive impressions, watch for the following three characteristics. The first is when impressions come in quickly, sometimes even before you can ask or complete a question. The second is when what you receive seems very odd to you, and you know it is not something you would have made up. The third is when you experience an absolute feeling of certainty about the information. If any one of these conditions is present, you can be fairly certain that the impressions came directly from the animal.

Linda Miller told me several stories that illustrate these three characteristics. Linda talked to a dog named Oscar about his cancer diagnosis and the fact that the attending veterinarian said Oscar had three weeks to live. Oscar told Linda, "That veterinarian is stupid!" This communication came in really quickly and Linda knew it had to be from the dog, as she wasn't thinking the vet was stupid at all and she thought it odd that the dog would say that. But it turned out that Oscar went on to live another year.

Linda interviewed another dog who was slated to have knee surgery. When she asked if he was worried about anything, he said he was worried about money. Linda thought that odd, as he belonged to a rather well-to-do family. She asked him why he was worried about money and he replied, "Because my owners are always talking about it." Through a few inquiries, Linda found out the dog was right. The dog's people were nervous about how much the upcoming surgery was going to cost and were discussing it constantly.

When Linda asked a cat named Smudge whether he liked his name, he gave her an emphatic "No!"

"Well, Smudge," she asked, "what would you prefer to be called?"

"Prince," he replied.

When she told Smudge's person that the cat didn't like his

name, the woman responded, "Oh, so he doesn't like his name, huh? I suppose he wants to be called His Royal Highness!"

Verifying Messages from Your Own Animals

When talking with your own animals, you will find it harder to get this kind of instant verification. I recommend instead focusing on getting a flow of conversation going. It is possible to get verification with your own animals, though, and when you do, it will often come in the form of some behavior that tells you they heard and understood you. Here are two examples.

Jo Spenser's dog, Rebel, is somewhat overprotective of her, so she decided to have a chat with him to prepare him for an upcoming birthday party. She told him that the people coming were friends and should be allowed to enter, and that he was not to try to intimidate them by barking or growling. As she was talking to Rebel, she got a feeling back from him that hit her, she said, "Smack, square in the middle of my brain." It was a feeling of him telling her that if they were going to have guests, he wanted to have a bath. Jo said Rebel was not the most cooperative about bathing, and since he weighs fifty-five kilograms, she thought she would probably end up getting soaked. But as she picked up the bottle of shampoo and towel, Rebel leapt up with the same excitement he normally displayed for going on walks. He then proceeded to be extremely cooperative, turning when necessary, and lifting his paws during the whole bathing event. He even moved away from her to shake, and there was no lead or collar in sight.

My horse trainer, Kelly Michalec, told me this story about her mustang, Guinness, who was taken from the wild at the age of four. He had started to get nippy with her. She couldn't figure out what the problem was, but she knew he was trying to tell her something. He was not in any obvious pain. She kept asking him, "Do your feet hurt? Does your back hurt? What's wrong?" Then one day, she asked, "Do your teeth hurt?" As soon as she said that, he stopped biting. Kelly knew that even though she had had his teeth worked on, there must still be a problem. She got the dentist out to recheck him, and they found that he had a broken baby tooth way in the back of his mouth. Guinness never tried to bite her again. If they had not discovered his broken tooth, it could have led to serious infection.

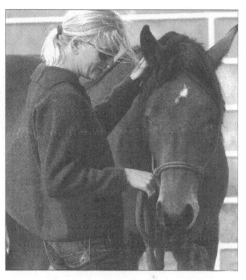

Kelly and Guinness

RECEIVING INFORMATION INTUITIVELY

The following exercises help you practice receiving information from your animals. Make sure you have your notebook when you do them so you can record your results. As you try these exercises, see which ones you like best and, if possible, find a way to do an exercise every day with your animal. To learn to communicate intuitively, you will have to find ways to practice regularly in your daily life.

Remember, you are already connected to your own animals. All you have to do is start communicating with them. However, to receive information, it does help to close your eyes. If you want, send a feeling of love to your animal before you start talking. And don't worry if your animal is moving around, eating, or playing when you communicate. It is not necessary that your animal pay attention to you. Nor does your animal have to be with you when you do these exercises; you can talk to your animal over any distance.

EXERCISE
What's Happening?

As you go about your day, whenever you have the feeling that your animal is trying to tell you something, stop and ask what it is. If nothing comes in, just tell your animal to keep trying and that you will get it eventually. Record any information you receive.

EXERCISE
What's Your Opinion?

Start to involve your animal more in your life by asking for his or her opinion. You can ask for an opinion on any area of your life — on anything that you are doing or planning to do. For example, you can ask what your animal thinks of one of your friends, or about which park to visit. Just ask out loud, "What is your opinion about [fill in the blank]?" Then record whatever impressions you receive.

EXERCISE
Ask for a Message

Send your animal a mental compliment, and then ask if your animal has a message for you. Record anything that comes in and accept it as coming from your animal.

EXERCISE
Ask for a Question

This is one of my favorite exercises. It just came to me one day when I was thinking how communicators are constantly asking animals questions. It occurred to me that animals might get tired of this. What if the animal had a question? How would it get answered? In this exercise, start by asking your animal if he or she has a question for you. Ask this out loud. Then pay close attention to see if a question pops into your mind. You can close your eyes or leave them open. Take the first question you are aware of, regardless of whether you think it could have come from your animal. Answer it as best you can. If you don't get a question, tell your animal that you will ask another day. If you do get a question, don't stop. Keep asking your animal for questions, answering them as best you can, until your animal stops asking questions.

The beauty of this exercise is that it lets your animal set the agenda and get his or her needs and concerns addressed. When you do this exercise, you may find yourself involved in a back-and-forth discussion of some issue that your animal brings up, and isn't that exactly what everyone hopes and dreams they could do?

Sometimes animals come up with some funny questions. One I will never forget occurred in a class I taught in Massachusetts. A woman asked her border collie for a question. The dog responded with a series of five questions, each time asking if the woman loved her as much as one of the other five border collies the woman owned. For each question the woman responded that of course she loved the dog as well as the other ones.

"Well," the dog asked as her final question, "If that's true, then do you love me enough to take me home now?"

Classic border collie behavior: Head 'em up, move 'em out.

CHAPTER 3
Pack of Two

I took the title for this chapter from a book by Caroline Knapp.[1] It is one of my favorite books and I recommend it to you. The author explores her relationship with a rescue dog and the depth of connection that develops as their lives intertwine. There are those animals in our lives — and it's not every one — who are our soul mates. Every day with such an animal is marked by joy and unconditional love.

The kind of relationship we can have with an animal is more profound than anything possible with another human because animals have qualities humans do not. They inhabit the present moment completely, in body, mind, heart, and spirit, bringing us with them, away from our focus on the future and the past. When we can join an animal in that present-tense world, time stands still and life completely involves us. Thus, walking the dog, playing with the cat, or feeding the horses turns into the most rewarding and restful part of the day.

Another characteristic that makes the human-animal relationship unique is the fact that animals do not and will not lie. If we pay attention, they tell us moment by moment, intuitively and through their body language, exactly how they feel about something we've done or something that has occurred. They give us honest, immediate feedback instead of dissembling and disconnecting from their hearts, the way people often do. Unless severely abused, animals are always acutely aware of their emotions and tend to immediately act upon them. Few humans operate this way. When you are with an animal you can always trust that you will hear the truth, if you choose to listen. Most humans are incapable of the unconditional love and unlimited capacity for forgiveness that animals offer, over and over. If we extend our love to an animal, we know it will eventually be returned tenfold. And we know that if we make mistakes but mean well, our animals are sure to forgive us. I define these qualities as the characteristics of an authentic being, and no matter how domesticated an animal may appear, he or she has all of these qualities in abundance. I believe both people and animals are born as authentic beings. The difference is that animals stay that way and we don't.

In most modern cultures, we are conditioned to disengage from our hearts, to focus on the past and the future to the exclusion of the present, and to think rather than feel. As we age, we learn to be judgmental, slow to forgive, and wary about extending love to one another. It's just the modern way, sadly. However, it was probably not this way in most ancient, indigenous cultures. I believe people of such cultures had the same authentic qualities as animals, and when growing up, they probably retained these qualities. In declaring animals to be more authentic than modern humans, I am not making them out to be angels. Animals do gross things; they kill, they eat poop, and they can be scary, frustrating, and stubborn. What I am asserting is that you will never catch an animal being phony, and you can pretty much count on an animal to forgive you for something for which a person might permanently reject you.

IT TAKES TWO

Our animals want nothing more from us than to be happy with them and with life. They want to form a pack of two with us, where we move and act as one. When the flow and connection are not present in our relationships with our animals, it can be instructive to discover why. If we have the courage to look, animals can become our greatest teachers. It can take time to create the pack we dream of having with our animal, but in that creation our lives are always enriched. As Suzanne Clothier put it in *Bones Would Rain from the Sky:*

> Each relationship with an animal and a human is a bridge uniquely shaped to carry only those two, and so must be crafted by them. Though the work of a lifetime, the building and repairs are done slowly, in the heart's time, one beat after another. And it is thirsty work, as work of the heart always is, for the heart thirsts after the things that are invisible to the eye, things you cannot grasp with your hand.[2]

Liam

When I rescued Liam, he was underweight and his feet were in horrible shape. His hip was out on the right side and his teeth needed work. Other than that, I was told, he was a well-trained horse and should be easy to manage. Within the first week, this well-trained horse was charging at me in the pasture and the barn aisle, and turning and bucking at me when I went into his stall. His whole attitude was one of extreme aggression. Did I mention that he is a Percheron draft horse who weighs about two thousand pounds? My reaction was disbelief that this horse, whom I had saved from the auction block, would be so ungrateful as to behave in this manner. I was also afraid of him and panicked about what to do. The person who gave him to me came and showed me some nonviolent natural horsemanship training techniques to get Liam to stop most of his aggressive behaviors, but underneath he was still seething. I could tell from the look in his eye that he did not think much of me, and he was certainly not pleased with his new life. In my early interactions with Liam, I had forgotten to take my own advice. I did not interview him intuitively to find out about his past. I didn't ask him daily for a question or to give me his opinion about something. I talked to him quite a lot, telling him what I wanted him to do, but I stayed stuck in — and solely concerned with — my experience and reality, to the exclusion of his.

When I finally found a horse trainer I wanted to work with, I was able to solve the puzzle of Liam. My new trainer declared, "He's scared. He doesn't know if you are going to put pressure on him and be unfair and unkind to him like everyone has been throughout his life. He expects you to be no different. You will have to use extreme patience, consistency, and love to turn him around." From that point on, I focused on Liam's reality instead of mine. I interviewed him and asked him what had happened to him in the past, and I heard his stories of the abuse he had gone through. He said he did not ever want to do ground work with a whip again and that he hated arenas. I promised him we would not do any of that. He was very unsure

Liam

about having his feet worked on, as people had always made them sore and had been mean to him on top of it. I promised him we would be careful. He wasn't sure he liked being ridden and wanted just to be left alone. I promised him he would not have to do anything he didn't like.

Through a combination of intuitive exchanges, gentle corrections, patience, and understanding, the true Liam slowly emerged. He needed to have the gentlest of approaches to be able to let down his defenses. Part of this may be because he is a draft horse, and they tend to be very sensitive and easily offended. His eyes got softer and softer, until now they are his most striking feature. Today he resembles nothing so much as a gigantic, black, contented dog. He has discovered that riding can be fun, and he is the first one to show up for attention when people visit the barn. In one of my beginning classes, I had the students talk to Liam. He told them, when asked about his feet, that I had given him "new feet" and he was very happy with them. Liam taught me that the only way to achieve the experience of the pack is through mutual respect. It wasn't just a matter of teaching him to respect me; I had to learn to respect him.

Star

Carla Abernathy's horse Star had a similar lesson for her. Carla was also being charged by her horse. She felt Star was not trying to harm her, but Star was upset and trying to tell her something. Star's sister, Sky, the lead mare of the herd, did not appreciate the disagreement going on between Star and Carla. Sky came up to them one day, made a sweep of her head from Carla to Star, and then bit the air. Carla said that inside her head she heard a clear voice say, "Get over it! Make up, you two!"

After Sky's urging, Carla decided to practice her animal communication skills on Star to find out what was bothering her. She interviewed Star about why she was

Carla and Star

mad, and she got the impression that she and her friend Kathy had hurt Star's feelings. Carla could feel sadness coming from Star. She got the sense that Star wanted an apology from Carla, and from Kathy, who had raised Star. Recently, Kathy had been so frustrated with Star for not standing still to mount that she had used a stern voice to vent her frustration, calling Star a stubborn, bull-headed pain in the butt. Both women apologized out loud to Star. Then Carla asked Star what she needed to help her be able to stand still. Carla received an image in her mind of Star standing on the grass and interpreted that as a message from Star that she wanted to stand in the grass, not on the cement. Then Carla received a feeling from Star that she was worried that someone would fall and get hurt, and Star felt safer having people get on her in the grass. That seemed to do the trick, because Star returned to her happy self once the mounting block was moved to the grass. Carla could have used a riding crop or some other device to make Star submit and behave, but she would have lost Star's trust in the process. Instead, she listened.

Annabelle

Here is another story of how one can create a much deeper and significant relationship with an animal through the use of intuitive communication. During the Hurricane Katrina disaster, Lorraine Smith rescued a dog who had been shipped from Louisiana to a local shelter. She named the dog Annabelle. Using holistic care (a combination of craniosacral work, a raw food diet, and energy healing), she helped Annabelle recover from severe emaciation and jaundice, and cleared up the sores on her body, even though the veterinarians at the shelter had given no hope of survival for the dog. Lorraine was elated by her success, but she soon realized that she had a serious problem with Annabelle, who had a high prey drive and would jump the fence to go after cats and other animals. Lorraine had to be realistic about what kind of life it would be for a dog to be confined inside a house for fifteen years or more. Euthanasia was becoming a possibility. She reasoned that there could be worse things than releasing the spirit from the body, and she made an appointment to put Annabelle down.

Lorraine spent every moment she could with Annabelle prior to the vet appointment. And she kept getting an intuitive nudge, telling her to go back and look at her decision again. She prayed for just one little fragment within Annabelle that she could work with. Finally, she sat down with the dog and said in a firm voice, "Look, little girl. Your life is on the line here, so you need to let me know now if there is a way we can change this." Lorraine took a few deep breaths and sat quietly with her eyes closed, being open to anything that might come in. Suddenly there was a connection, and it felt to Lorraine like she was talking to a very wise spirit who was watching over Annabelle. The shift was undeniable, and the spirit gave Lorraine clear instructions for what needed to be done.

Annabelle could stay and things would work out only if Lorraine agreed to keep her safe, protect her at all times, and be totally committed to helping her. A contract was made. Then Lorraine sought out a good trainer and finally found one who could help through positive training methods. From then on, they never looked back, and Annabelle is a different dog today. She even received her AKC Canine Good Citizen Certificate, and she is very good at agility. She likes to attend group obedience classes to show the other dogs how it's done. But Lorraine always has

*Lorraine and her dogs,
Jade (left) and Annabelle*

to be aware that Annabelle has issues and can never be put in a situation where she could feel unsafe and make the wrong decision.

Midnight

Being able to communicate intuitively with your animal allows you to have dialogues together, which is something every animal person would love to be able to do. This happened for Janice Camp after she took one of my classes. When Janice returned home, she visited her mare, Midnight. Janice sensed that Midnight was worried, so she asked her what was wrong. Instantly, a wave of anguish and sadness welled up. Even though the feelings were coming from Midnight,

Janice started to cry. She asked Midnight what the sadness was about. Midnight let Janice know that she was worried that Janice would get rid of her because she was lame. Janice reassured Midnight that she was her horse for life, no matter what happened. But Midnight replied that the other people who had sold her did so because she was lame.

Janice and Midnight then got into a bit of an argument. Janice said, "No, Midnight. I won't get rid of you, ever." Midnight said, "Yes, you will!" Janice said, "I am going to win this argument!" Midnight looked straight at Janice. Then she nodded, once. As *Janice and Midnight* quickly as it had started, it was over. Midnight seems fine now, and because Janet has learned how to communicate with her, she can keep on checking that the mare is okay.

FINDING YOUR PACK

Now that I have become more conscious of my relationships with animals, I have noticed a trend. It appears that all my animals find *me*, rather than me finding them. This is true

even when I go in search of a particular type of animal. For example, I decided one day, for no obvious reason, that I wanted to have a kitten. I always had plenty of cats, so I didn't need a new one. But the desire took hold. I was considering going to the shelter when one of my students told me that she had some barn kitties, and one of them looked like a skunk. Well, that was all it took. I happen to love skunks, so I had to go check out the kitten. Once I did, I had to have her. I'm pretty sure though, that the whole thing was really Phoebe's idea.

Phoebe as a kitten

In this story from my friend Sherry Gregory, it is hard to argue that there wasn't something more going on. Like me, Sherry had been thinking that she wanted a new animal — in her case, a little dog. She woke up each morning thinking about the dog. Then the name "Flower" started to come to her, and she decided she would call the dog Flower. One day she made plans to go look for the dog. She checked the paper and found a local place that had Jack Russell terriers. That felt right, so she called the breeder and said she wanted a broken-coat (long-haired) Jack Russell and nothing else. The breeder said that she had just one broken-coat dog, and it wasn't for sale. Sherry said that was all she was interested in, but the breeder coaxed her into coming to look at the puppies anyway. The puppies were cute, but as Sherry stood watching them, something made her turn and look about forty feet away at a pick-up truck. There she saw a little head pop up. "Who's that?" she asked the breeder. "That's Flower," the woman said. Sherry told her that she had to have the dog. Afterward, the breeder said she had known, when Sherry

Sherry and Flower

talked to her on the phone, that Sherry would be taking Flower home. Flower turned out to be a severely abused dog who needed a safe home with lots of love. Now she and Sherry belong to each other.

Cindy Courson-Brown couldn't stop herself from buying her horse Penny. She was at an auction, and when she looked at Penny, she felt something she has never felt with anyone or anything. Her hand went up in the air to bid and stayed there, even though her husband kept asking her to stop. She would not be out-bid. From the moment she took Penny home, she and the horse were able to freely talk back and forth intuitively.

However, at the time Cindy attended one of my workshops, their relationship was troubled, and Cindy was concerned about Penny. Penny appeared to be pregnant and quite round, but nothing was happening and she was well past her due date. In addition, Cindy could no longer hear Penny talking to her. Penny had completely shut down. Before leaving for the workshop, Cindy made an appointment with the veterinarian to come check Penny out. At the end of the workshop Cindy planned to ask me to talk to Penny and find out about the baby. But then she heard a small, sad voice say, "I lost the baby." The next day, the veterinarian confirmed what Cindy had heard intuitively. That evening, Cindy went to see Penny,

Cindy and Penny

and put her arms around her and held her. She could feel Penny's emotion. She reassured Penny that losing the baby didn't change how much she loved her. After that, Penny started to talk to Cindy again, and they regained their close connection.

CREATING THE BOND

No matter how many animals you have, life with an animal always comes down to the minute-by-minute interaction you have together. Ask yourself whether in each moment that you are with your animal you are creating the relationship you want to have. If not, listen to your animal and commit to finding your way toward trust, respect, and love. Believe it is possible and pursue it with all your heart. Here are some intuitive tools that can help.

EXERCISE
Telling

One tool for creating the bond you want is to express your desires to your animal while holding the belief that your animal completely understands what you are saying. You can talk out loud or send thoughts mentally to your animal.

Marilyn Terry tried this one day with her Peruvian Paso horse, Cancion. Marilyn does not regularly ride Cancion, but one spring day she took him from the pasture and decided it would be nice to see how he would react to having her on his back again. His demeanor told her it would be okay, but she was nervous about it, since he had been confined in the paddock for a while and had not been ridden for some time. As she brushed and saddled him, she talked to him mentally and out loud. He seemed quiet, but she knew that with him that could be the calm before the storm. She told

him, "You are a very big boy, and you weigh much more than I do. You can really hurt me if you want. I am all alone with you, and there's no one to help me if you do not take care of me. So, I'm trusting you to take really good care of me."

As she spoke with him, she felt connected and knew that everything would be all right; she knew intuitively

Marilyn and Cancion

that he understood. She stood on a barrel to get on his back, and he stood absolutely still, as if rooted to the ground. Once she was on his back, he turned and nosed at the foot she had been too nervous to slip into the stirrup. He did not move until she told him to, and then he walked slowly around the paddock as if she were fragile china on his back. He did exactly what Marilyn asked, and she could tell that he was filled with a sense of pride and confidence at what he was doing. It was for both of them a moment of true connection.

EXERCISE
Listening

It is equally important to begin listening to your animal. Ask your animal the questions listed below and listen for his or her answer. Remember to go with the first impressions that come to you. Record them in your notebook. If nothing is coming in, make a good guess for each of the questions below and record that in your notebook. See if you notice any changes in your animal's behavior over time that might constitute proof that what you received intuitively from your animal was accurate. Make a note of these confirmations.

- What do you like about me, and why?
- What do I do that bugs you, and why?
- What do you like about your life, and why?
- What would you like changed, and why?
- What, if anything, are you worried about, and why?
- What, if anything, do you need, and why?

EXERCISE
Discovering Your Purpose Together

You can deepen your relationship by asking your animal the questions below. Remember to go with the first impressions that come to you. Record them in your notebook. If nothing is coming in, force yourself to make a good guess for each of the questions below and record that in your notebook.

- What is your purpose in my life?
- What are you teaching me?
- What is my purpose in your life?
- What am I teaching you?

CHAPTER 4
Creating the Peaceable Kingdom

Your home is meant to be a place of peace and comfort. When members of your household aren't getting along, be they human or animal, it makes for ongoing, unpleasant stress that can adversely affect everyone's health and well-being. Intuitive techniques can go a long way toward resolving conflict and creating the peaceable kingdom we'd like to have in our homes.

Here is an example of how this can work from my own experience. One day, my horse trimmer, Tiffany Ashcraft, convinced me to rescue just one more horse to add to the three rescued horses I already had. Mackey was a paint horse who had lost one of his beautiful blue eyes to cancer. Tiffany rescued him from a situation where he'd been in a muddy pasture all by himself. She put him with her horses temporarily, but couldn't keep him. I was worried that my horses wouldn't accept Mackey and might attack him on his blind side. I was also concerned that Mackey might get depressed because he had been befriended by one of Tiffany's horses and would now have to leave his new friend. I got even more worried when seasoned horse people told me it could take a month or more for my horses to accept a new horse. I didn't want Mackey to be lonely and stressed for that long. So I decided that it wasn't going to happen that way.

The first thing I did was stay positive and calm. Despite what everyone told me, I was going to expect the best of the situation. I envisioned for myself that my horse Liam, the herd leader, would be nice to Mackey, and that Rio, my other gelding, would become the best of friends with Mackey. I pictured all this happening and let myself feel how great it would be if things turned out that way. Then I talked with all my horses. I told them what was happening, explained that Mackey was blind on one side, and asked them to accept him and take care of him. I especially asked Liam to be kind to Mackey. I visualized for them what I wanted and how I wanted them to act.

When we brought Mackey in, I kept him apart from the other horses for a day. When we introduced him to the herd, Rio went after Mackey and chased him away, but Liam left him

Liam, Isabelle, and Rio (Mackey is in the background, barely visible)

alone. I praised Liam for being calm and kind, as I had asked him to do. After four days, Mackey worked his way to the edge of the herd and could eat hay without being challenged. Then I told the horses that as soon as they accepted Mackey, they could get back into the barn aisle, where they like to hang out during the day. Every time Mackey got chased off, I reminded the horses that the sooner they accepted him, the sooner life would return to normal. By the end of the week, rather than the predicted one month, I was able to open the gate to the barn aisle, and all four horses stood in the barn without incident. After another week, Mackey had almost completely integrated into the herd; he was playing with Rio and obviously happy with his new life.

INTUITIVE TECHNIQUES FOR CREATING THE PEACEABLE KINGDOM

The intuitive techniques I used to introduce Mackey to the herd are described in detail below. These techniques are sometimes all that is needed to create harmony between animals. But some situations can best be addressed through a combination of intuitive techniques and training or other approaches. Each situation requires different strategies. For example, a dog who has been attacked in the past and has developed fear and aggression toward other dogs would probably need a combination of strategies. Keep in mind, as you read through these intuitive techniques, that the underlying premise for each is that your animals can perceive and understand all your words, thoughts, and feelings.

Adopt a Calm, Positive Attitude

How you feel has a big influence on how your animals behave. If you are introducing a new animal to your household, or are trying to get two warring animals to get along better, you have to believe that the outcome will be good. You need to create a positive, calm feeling in yourself and project that into the situation. The techniques below can help you manifest the positive change you want:

1. Breathe — If you find yourself becoming worried and having negative expectations, focus on breathing and releasing the tension, worry, or negative thoughts. Take a breath, then along with your exhalation, relax any place that is tense in your body. Do this for a few minutes until you feel calmer.
2. Cancel negative thoughts — If you become aware of negative thoughts about your animals, such as feeling that there will be a fight or an injury, catch yourself and mentally give yourself a command to cancel that thought.
3. Substitute a positive phrase — Replace your negative thought with a positive phrase you can repeat to yourself

whenever you like. For example, you could say, "Everything is going smoothly and peacefully." As you go about the day, repeat your positive phrase whenever you think about your animals. Keep your thoughts focused on a positive result.

Talk and Ask

Explain to your animals what you want them to do and how you want them to behave. Ask for their cooperation. Be as specific and detailed as possible. Include an explanation of how you are feeling, why you feel as you do, and why you want the result you are asking for. In other words, talk to them about the situation in the same way you would talk to a friend or family member. You can do this out loud or just send the information mentally.

Show Mental Movies

Animals can mentally "see" the images we form in our minds. When you are working to create a certain behavior in your animal, show the behavior as an image in your mind. Make a mental movie showing your animal what your dream is — what you hope will happen. Make this movie as real and detailed as possible. Enjoy making the movie and feel how great it would be if it could actually come true. Place yourself as an actor in the mental movie and feel as if you are living what you are imagining. Making the idea as real as possible is what makes it actually happen. Your animal will see and feel along with you as you make the mental movie. Make sure it is always positive and always feels good when you are doing it.

Offer Reminders and Prevent Mistakes

Remind your animals by telling them out loud what you are expecting of them. For example, I reminded my lead horse, Liam, that I expected him to be a good, kind herd leader, to be fair to Mackey, and to realize that Mackey could not see on one side. But

I also locked all the horses out of the barn aisle at first to make sure they didn't get crowded in and lash out at Mackey as a result. This prevented the horses from making a mistake as they accommodated a new animal in a confined space. Look for any circumstances that have the potential for creating unnecessary conflict, and change them, at least temporarily.

Offer Incentives

The incentive I offered my horses was the return of access to the barn aisle. Liam in particular likes to loaf in the barn when it is hot, to get away from the horse flies and the heat. By closing off the barn, I was taking away an important resource. I continually reminded him that the sooner he and the rest of them accepted Mackey and acted nice to him, the sooner they could go back in the barn.

Time-Out and Lecture

When I was introducing Mackey to the herd, every so often my Arab, Rio, would charge him, just on general principles it seemed. I was concerned that Rio was jealous. I took him aside a few times and talked to him about the situation. I explained that just like Rio, Mackey was a rescue who didn't have a good home and needed one. I asked Rio to try to be understanding and at least tolerate Mackey. Whenever Rio was particularly nasty to Mackey, I followed this lecture with a short time-out period away from the herd, to think about how he would do things differently.

Compliments for Progress

We all like to be told we are doing well. Animals are no different. If you see the slightest bit of improvement or cooperation, it is essential to praise your animal to the roof for it. I also like to give jackpot rewards for really great progress. Just make sure to tell your animals exactly why they are getting all those carrots or doggie treats.

Another Case Study

Karen Berke told me this story of how intuitive communication helped facilitate harmony among her five cats. Karen likes to hone her skills by attending my practice groups. At one session, she asked the group to talk with her cats, who had a long-standing problem of not getting along well. Bootsie, a black-and-white male, was the main cause. He liked to harass her other cats, particularly Sparkey, a male gray tabby. Bootsie would relentlessly chase Sparkey, and whenever Bootsie was around, Sparkey was wary. All the people in the practice group spoke to both cats, offering the cats advice and encouragement for better relations.

Karen emailed me after the practice to tell me that when she got home, Sparkey came walking into the kitchen to greet her, followed by Bootsie. That had never happened before. If Bootsie was anywhere outside the door, Sparkey would not come in until the coast was clear. Later that evening, as she was watching TV, Bootsie came up to lie next to her. Then Snoopy, another of her cats, jumped up. And then, to her great surprise, Sparkey came into the room. He looked at her, and she told him it was okay to come up. Then he, too, jumped up to lie next to her. This was also something that had never happened before.

EXERCISE
Creating the Peaceable Kingdom

Here is a summary of the intuitive techniques to follow to create a peaceable kingdom.

- Be positive that the conflict can be resolved. Cancel negative thoughts and substitute positive ones.
- Talk to your animals in depth about the problems and how you feel. Then ask them to behave in the manner you desire.
- Show them mental movies of how you want things to be.
- Expect the best.

- Remind your animals of what they need to do, and set things up so they can't fail.
- Negotiate and offer incentives, if needed.
- Take a time-out and give a lecture for bad behavior.
- Give compliments and treats for progress.
- Try out other complementary techniques (see the Resources section, page 183).

As always, record in your notebook what you are doing and track any impressions you receive and any changes that occur. If your animals comply with your requests, thank and praise them.

OTHER TECHNIQUES FOR CREATING PEACE

There are several other techniques for addressing conflicts and encouraging animals to get along. Animal training methods that avoid the use of force and punishment, like clicker training,[1] can be helpful. For a complete description and guides to these techniques, see the Resources section (page 183). Here are some things that I have tried and can recommend.

- Herbs — I recently introduced a new cat to my other cats. I used all the intuitive techniques I know, but just to hedge my bets, I tried a suggestion I found online: I covered all the cats with catnip before introducing the new cat. I don't know if that is what did it, since I tried a lot of things at once, but I had a very easy time integrating that new cat into my home.
- Behavioral tricks — Some other ideas that I found online were to exchange sleeping blankets and bowls while keeping the cats separated to get them used to each other's scent, and to let them see each other through a screen or glass door before the introductions. These techniques worked very well.

- Flower essences — Essences were developed for people but are now used for animals as well. Essences address emotional conditions and have a subtle but observable effect.
- Holistic health care — Whatever the issue, switching the animal to the best holistic diet and health care will improve the animal's attitude and behavior. A holistic vet can do acupuncture, homeopathy, and chiropractic, all of which make an animal feel better and thus act better.
- Energy healing — There are many kinds of energy healing, but all of them are based on the idea that our bodies are energy, and when energy is flowing freely, we are healthy and relaxed. Energy healing can help ease tension between animals and can help an animal release negative emotions from the past.
- Massage — There are many styles of massage and body work that can be done for animals to restore balance to the body and encourage a calmer, more comfortable, and happier animal.

CHOOSING A NEW ANIMAL

You can use intuitive techniques to determine an animal's personality and suitability for your household, and to get a sense of whether the animal will get along with and be accepted by others, or whether a different animal might be better in terms of sex, age, or personality.

Gerrie Huijts, a professional animal communicator, uses the following technique for determining the fitness of a new animal for a client's home. Gerrie regularly gets requests from people who want help in choosing a new dog, cat, or horse. Besides the obvious emotional consequences of choosing unwisely, there can be a lot of money involved — in the case of buying a new horse especially. To see if the new animal is appropriate for the home, Gerrie asks the client to write a letter to the new animal, stating what is expected from the animal and what the animal can expect in return. She encourages the client to include expectations regarding personality, likes, dislikes, care, breeding, and relationships with other animals in the household. Gerrie then reads this letter to the animal, and asks what he or she expects from the new home and person. From this she can determine if the proposed adoption will be a match, and whether the animal wants to live with the person or not and why.

Gerrie and her dog Niki

Talking with an Animal You Don't Know

To use communication to evaluate an animal you are thinking of adopting, you need to learn how to talk with an animal you don't know. Communicating with an animal you don't know is essentially the same as communicating with your own animals; you can just send love, start talking, and then pay attention to every impression that comes to you. However, when introducing yourself to an animal that is completely unknown to you, you may find it helps to spend a little more time focusing and connecting before you start communicating. Here are the techniques for doing that.

First, use your breathing to relax and clear your mind. Keep breathing and releasing until you feel completely relaxed. Then open to your intuition. Be open to all the ways intuitive impressions can come to you through seeing, hearing, feeling, knowing, smelling, and tasting. Set yourself up for success by saying something like, "I'm really good at this."

Envision the animal in your mind. You don't have to see the animal in person; you can form an image using a description or a photograph. Focus on a mental image of the animal and turn your attention inward. Before you begin talking, record any first impressions that are coming to you about the animal. Search for any impressions that come into your awareness, whether you think they are obvious, made-up, inaccurate, silly, or stupid. Take every single thing that comes in and record it all until there is no more information.

Once you have finished gathering first impressions, imagine being in the presence of the animal, as if the animal were right there in front of you. Introduce yourself, explain what you are doing, and ask for the animal's help. If it feels okay to proceed — if the animal seems either neutral or interested and positive — then keep going. If the animal seems worried or uncomfortable, explain in more detail what you want to do. Ask why the animal is uncomfortable and see if you can resolve the issue. If not, just say thanks and disengage. You can try again later to see if you can make a connection with the animal.

If the animal is okay with talking, imagine that you and the animal are together in whatever surroundings you choose. If it is okay for both you and the animal, interact with the animal as if you were together. Give the animal a pat or a treat. Go on an imaginary adventure with the animal if you like. Give the animal a compliment. When you are completely comfortable, you can begin asking the animal your questions and have a dialogue. It won't matter if you speak English and the animal you are talking with has only been around people speaking some other language. Intuitive communication is the universal language, so there is instantaneous translation among and between all languages and all beings. When you are finished talking, thank the animal.

EXERCISE
Choosing a New Animal

Here is a summary of the process for talking with an animal you don't know. If you are planning to adopt a new animal, try this exercise for interviewing the animal intuitively before making the decision to adopt.

- First get the name, age, and description of the animal (you can work with the animal in person or from a distance).
- Breathe and relax. Be open to all intuitive impressions: sounds, thoughts, feelings, hunches, images, smells, and tastes.
- Close your eyes, focus on the animal, and record all your first impressions.
- Now, imagine being in the presence of the animal. Introduce yourself, explain what you are doing, and make sure it feels okay to proceed.
- If it is okay with the animal, imagine interacting with the animal; petting the animal and even going on an adventure together.
- Now you can ask your questions. For example, ask the animal how he or she would feel about coming to live with you, and record your results.
- If you have other animals, imagine all the animals being together, and pay attention to what your impressions tell you about their potential feelings for each other and interactions. Record your results.
- Ask whatever other questions you have and record your results.
- When you are finished, tell the animal thank you.

INTRODUCING NEW ANIMALS TO EACH OTHER

I've already described the situation in which I introduced a new horse into my herd; here are two more case studies of introducing new animals into a household. A few years ago, Irene Bras, who lives in the Netherlands and practices animal communication professionally, came across a picture of a small, traumatized dog, Deva, on the Internet. The dog had been rescued from death in a shelter by a rescue organization and had been brought to the Netherlands, where she was staying with a foster family. When Irene saw the dog, she felt an immediate connection. But she had her own animals to think of; how would they feel about a new family member? She introduced Deva to her animals intuitively, and they talked things over. Everybody agreed, and so Deva came to live with them. Irene said Deva felt at home from the very beginning and was completely accepted by her other animals.

Melina Wakefield also used intuitive techniques to introduce a new dog into her household. The catch is that she introduced two adult male Chow Chows to each other. Chows can be dog-aggressive, and probably no trainer in his or her right mind would have recommended that she do this. Melina had one Chow named Shambo. She met the second Chow while at a practice group I taught at a local humane society. She felt a strong attraction to the cream-colored dog, who was up for adoption, and she wanted to take him home.

First she used her intuitive communication skills to check out the situation. She told the dog that he would have to get along with Shambo and asked if he wanted to come live with them. She said she felt a wave of warmth from him and heard him ask, "Now? Can we go now?" Then he sent her an image of himself and Shambo walking through the redwood trees. He also told Melina that his name was Bear. Melina filled out the adoption papers, but it was too late in the day to take him home and introduce him to Shambo, so she told Bear she would be back the next morning.

Melina went home and talked to Shambo about it. He told her he had some reservations but would be willing to meet Bear and try it out. She assured Shambo he would always be the top dog. The next day she went with Shambo to meet Bear. She mentally explained to each what was expected of them and that she wanted them to be respectful pack mates. Under the nervous eye of a humane society trainer, the two hefty males met, sniffed each other, and went about their business. So Bear came home. Melina reminded Bear that Shambo was always first, and she cautioned him to respect Shambo and his food. She mentally showed Bear their daily routines and what he would be expected to do. Bear settled in as if he had been there forever, and the dogs got on well together from the start.

ANIMAL-HUMAN CONFLICTS

The techniques I have described above can also be used to address conflicts between humans and animals, as this next story demonstrates. After Triny Fischer's dog Nora died, she decided to adopt another dog. Triny and her husband picked out Duke, a fourteen-year-old German shepherd with hip dysplasia. Duke had been in foster care for two years, and they adopted him because they knew no one else would.

About four days after Duke's arrival, the first biting incident occurred. Triny's husband, a big man with a loud voice, came into the kitchen while Triny was cooking, and he bent down to kiss Duke. Duke instantly bit him in the face. They were shocked. How could that sweet dog have done that? The days that followed were very stressful. Her husband was angry and scared. Duke was a nervous wreck, and Triny felt responsible for the whole mess. She immediately set kitchen boundaries for Duke, but when her husband tried to discipline Duke, Duke attempted to bite him again. Many heated arguments ensued. In desperation, Triny called me. When I connected with Duke intuitively, he told me that he had never had enough food, and that he had been beaten by an alcoholic man who was loud and aggressive. Duke said he had learned to bite for protection, and it had become an automatic response.

I recommended that Triny use nonviolent training methods to teach Duke to be calmer. I also suggested working with a holistic veterinarian to try different modalities, including herbs, massage, a whole-food diet, energy healing, and flower essences. Most importantly, I recommended that her husband keep his voice low and calm, and that he and Duke talk about the situation. I advised him to explain his feelings and intentions, assure Duke that he would be safe, and talk to Duke about what he hoped and dreamed their relationship could be. Her husband reluctantly agreed to all this and agreed to take Duke to an obedience course. Eight months later, Duke was like a different dog. Triny says she can see that he is healing from his past trauma, and the change in him is amazing. Duke and her husband are doing fine, and Duke is now a favorite character in the neighborhood.

CHAPTER 5
Adding Intuition to Animal Training

*M*y horse trainer, Kelly Michalec, told me about a mare she was asked to help train. The mare was a show horse who had always been kept in a stall. The new owners were afraid to turn the mare out with other horses because of the way she was behaving. In order to halter or handle her, they had to use a whip, as she would lunge at people with her ears back and her teeth bared. Kelly started her training by standing next to the stall just out of the mare's reach, reading a book for hours. Kelly spoke out loud to the mare, informing her that she was going to stand outside the stall and not come in unless the mare stopped lunging at her.

In the first session, the mare lunged until she was exhausted, while Kelly just read her book and ignored her. Kelly returned a second time and again stood outside the stall and told the mare the same thing. This time, the mare stopped lunging fairly quickly, but hung back in the stall and was reactive whenever Kelly moved. The mare's ears were now forward though, and she seemed interested in Kelly. In the third training session, Kelly again stood by the stall with her book. She told the mare that if she could be polite, she would come in and visit her. The mare seemed calm and interested this time and walked right up to the door of the stall. Kelly opened the door and the mare came quietly up to her, lowered her head, and nickered. Then she stretched out her nose to touch Kelly's stomach. At the time Kelly was a few months pregnant.

After that, the mare became easy to handle and could be turned out with other mares. She is fine now, living in a herd and having a more natural lifestyle. She did try to steal one of the other mare's babies, though. Many horse trainers, even the natural ones, would have used some kind of force to try to get that mare to behave. What Kelly did instead was to take a nonforceful leadership role and use intuition to explain to the mare what she wanted her to do. Animals just want to be in harmony with us and do what we ask of them, within reason. The trick is how to get there.

LISTEN FIRST, THEN TRAIN

Most of the animal-training practices considered good and normal in our world do not take the animal's viewpoint into account. Animals should have the right to participate, and to have a say, in their training. According to Kelly, the true goal of training should be to get animals to do something because they want and choose to, not because we force them to. Instead, people typically get so involved in doing a program or getting a result — like winning the next title in a dog show — or they worry so much about getting hurt, that they fail to listen to what their animals have to say. That's when I get calls about the dogs who are refusing to go in the show ring or the horses who are acting crazy.

If you change your goal from requiring that your animals listen to you to instead listening to and loving your animals, you will change the dynamic. The instructions and exercises in chapter 2 for how to communicate intuitively with your animals will help you to become an expert at listening to animals. Talking to your animals every day as if they completely understand you changes the playing field: everyone becomes equal. Talking out loud to your animals also helps you to keep your breathing relaxed and to stay in the present moment, so that your body language, expertly read by your animal, aligns with what you are saying.

Tiffany Ashcraft, who encouraged me to rescue my horse Mackey, is called a natural or barefoot trimmer because she doesn't put shoes on horses, and she uses a technique of trimming horses' hooves that makes the hooves similar to those of wild horses. Most people don't yet know about this technique, as it is a new field, but it is part of the rapidly growing trend toward natural holistic care for horses. When done correctly, the barefoot trim helps horses stay comfortable, prevents lameness, and aids in their overall health and well-being; trimming should be done about every six weeks, just as we cut our nails. If the feet are not trimmed, problems can develop.

Tiffany was called in to work with a herd of mini horses (which are about one-eighth the size of a normal horse) who were having serious problem with lameness. When she went to work on the first mini, the horse reared and started to panic. The owner told Tiffany that the previous farrier (a person who shoes horses), had reacted to the horses' rearing by following the rear, flipping the minis all the way over, holding them down on the ground, and trimming their feet in that position. The minis were in a complete panic the entire time.

Tiffany decided she was not going to continue that tradition. Instead, she stopped everything she was doing and just listened to the minis and responded to what she was sensing from them. She promised them that she would never flip them over and hold them down. She sat on the ground with them and let them come up and visit. She promised them that if they pulled back, she would always release their feet and let them go. She also sent them mental visualizations of how she would do their feet, showing them that they would have complete control of the situation. Then, from a sitting position, she started to work with one of the minis. She gently pressed the back of the horse's foot and asked if she could have it. The horse yielded but then immediately panicked. Tiffany quickly let go of the foot, took a deep breath, and went back to sitting quietly. It took a while, but now Tiffany can trim all the minis at that barn with ease. They actually run to see her when she comes to visit, and they stand quietly and confidently while she does their feet. All their lameness issues were resolved by the switch to the barefoot trim. Tiffany and I used the same methods with my herd of horses, who were also quite wary of having their feet done.

It is actually common for horses to be difficult when it comes to trimming their feet. Their bad behavior can almost always be traced back to something that happened when they were getting their feet trimmed: either a farrier was mean to them and hit them, or what the farrier did ended up making the horse lame.[1] One of my horses in particular, a mare named Isabelle, was almost like a wild horse. She had been a brood mare all her life, producing baby after baby, and had never been ridden or very well cared for. Her feet had been done little, if at all, in her life. A previous owner had been observed chasing her for hours in an attempt to get her feet trimmed. Her attitude was "Forget you guys!" It took Tiffany and me a year to get Isabelle to the point where she would let us do all four feet with no fear or worry. We did it the same way, one foot at a time, letting her have her foot back, assuring her we would not hurt her, and visualizing her standing calmly while her feet got trimmed. The nonstop treats she gets when we do her feet probably also played a part in winning her trust and cooperation.

Tiffany and her horse Butterfly

BE A GOOD LEADER

To be successful at training you need to learn to be a good leader, the way Kelly was when she was training that aggressive mare. I believe that natural, nonviolent training methods are the best way to train animals. For example, if you needed to train a dog who is dog-aggressive, I would recommend the nonaggressive clicker training approach described in Emma Parsons's book *Click to Calm*,[2] rather than the dominance approach to dog training that you see portrayed a lot on TV. Being physically dominant to an animal works and you get obedience, but you don't get understanding and mutual respect. What makes a good leader? The horse in Mark Rashid's book *Life Lessons from a Ranch Horse*[3] is a good leader, respected by the other horses in his herd. He is consistent, fair, nonviolent, safe to be with, and sets clear boundaries. He is the perfect role model for a leader, and we could all do well to emulate his behavior. To understand what it takes to be a good leader with dogs, I recommend you read Jan Fennell's book *The Dog Listener*,[4] wherein she explores leadership from the point of view of the dog and gives valuable advice to humans wishing to be pack leaders to their dogs without resorting to violence and dominance. These lessons in leadership should be applied to cats as well, for the absence of clear boundaries with cats can result in being slashed and bitten.

SELECTING A TRAINING METHOD

Each animal is different, so when selecting a training method you can't take a cookie-cutter approach. This is where your intuition will serve you well. Using the intuitive communication skills you've developed so far in this book, you can find out what your animal thinks, feels, and needs, which will help you select the best training program for your animal.

If you're not sure what training method to use, check out the Resources section (page 183), where I list the training methods that I have found most helpful. If you already have a training method you like, then you can add the following intuitive training techniques to it to improve your success.

INTUITIVE TRAINING METHODS

Combining intuitive communication with nonviolent animal training methods can be highly effective in achieving training goals and establishing a good leadership dynamic with your animal. You can use intuitive communication to show, as well as tell, an animal what you want. One technique is to take your animal to a place where he can see another animal doing what you want him to do, such as taking your dog to watch an agility trial, or taking your horse to watch a jumping event. Add another intuitive layer by explaining to your animal, step-by-step, out loud or mentally, each aspect of the behavior as you are watching it. Tell your animal how he can accomplish the behavior; explain what he has to do in terms of timing and moving his body. Then try doing the behavior with him. You may find that just by letting him observe a behavior first, his learning ability will improve.

Another way to show your animal how you want him to act is to make the mental movie I described in chapter 4. First explain to your animal what you want and why. Then make the movie by simply closing your eyes and imagining your animal doing exactly what you want. See the scene as if it were happening, with you right there with your animal.

Gerrie Huijts, my colleague, checks in intuitively with her cats every morning when they go outside to find out what time they will be returning in the evening. They tell her the time, 8 or 11 P.M. or whatever, and they always appear at the specified time. Her cats also spontaneously trained themselves to be her backup alarm clock on the days when she has to get up really early. She got in the habit of turning off her alarm, falling back asleep, and then scrambling to get ready. A few times, she missed her train and had major problems. Now if she turns off her alarm and falls back asleep, her cats wake her up within fifteen minutes.

Tess

My student Carol Stoddard used intuitive talking and visualization in place of formal training aids when she rode her now-deceased endurance trail horse Tess, a registered Anglo-Arab. Carol first discovered she could do this with Tess when they were riding in the Vermont Green Mountain Horse Association 100 Mile Ride, considered to be the toughest three-day, hundred-mile endurance course event. She and Tess were alone on the trail, peacefully walking along, when Carol heard a voice ask, "May we trot now?" Without thinking she responded with a telepathic "Yes," and Tess took off in a trot. From that day on, Carol and Tess communicated telepathically. Tess would inform her when she wanted to trot or gallop on the trail, and Carol went along for the ride. If Carol wanted to change gaits, all she had to do was think "trot," and instantly they were trotting, or "canter" and they would be in a canter. The time between the thought and the actual transition into the gait was lightning fast. Carol did not consciously give any aids or clues to get Tess to speed up. Tess was an incredible athlete, at-

Tess and Carol

tacking and devouring the Vermont miles and hills, always placing in the top awards. She was one of the only horses ever to earn a perfect 100-point score in the Vermont event.

Troubleshooting

Intuition can come in handy whenever you find yourself stuck in a training situation. Checking in intuitively with the animal can sometimes help to resolve an impasse or move to the next level in your training process. Cindi Clarke, a client of mine, found herself at an impasse with her dog Trooper, who had been traumatized by men in the past. Trooper was acting afraid of men and other dogs. He just didn't have the self-confidence that a big dog should have.

Cindi used her intuition to come up with a plan to help him.

She decided to take him to two sessions of guard-dog training to rebuild his confidence, and it worked well. His fear level decreased when he was able to charge and chase off the "bad" man with the stick in the training session. Since she didn't want him to become an aggressive dog, just an assertive dog, she stopped after a few sessions. Now, each day when she leaves for work, she tells Trooper that

Cindi and Trooper (on left)

it is his job to keep the house safe and protect the other dog, a pug named Tink, and the cats. Trooper's self-confidence has grown, and he has learned to stand his ground when other dogs challenge him, rather than getting scared and running away. When this first happened at an animal day-care center, Trooper and the dog who was challenging him seemed to just trade titles without any fighting. Trooper came home that day a much more confident dog.

Neil and one of his horses

Neil Flood, who rides high-level dressage performance horses, provides another example. Like Carol, Neil says he has found that intuitive communication is sometimes more effective in handling horses than a trainer's instruction. He told me about an incident when a huge thoroughbred/warmblood mare he was riding started acting up. Every time he gave her a leg cue, she would swing around, dance, and act as if she were about to bolt.

Using intuitive communication, and firmly believing that it is never the horse's fault, he asked her what in the world he was doing wrong. He heard back from her intuitively (in words that came as a mental message) that her right ribs were bruised, and she asked if he could move his leg forward a bit. Neil adjusted his leg and she immediately started performing beautifully.

The Coach Approach

When training your animal I recommend taking what I call the Coach Approach. That means that you consider yourself to be your animal's coach and your animal is like your Olympic hopeful. No matter what anyone else says or does, most importantly a trainer, you have to believe that your animal can do whatever task you've set for yourselves. You have to believe in your animal 100 percent and say that to your animal. Tell your animal you will do whatever it takes to provide support.

EXERCISE
The Coach Approach

The Coach Approach builds on the intuitive tools you learned in the last chapter. Give it a try with one of your animals and see how it works. Here are the steps:

1. Believe that your animal is capable of doing what you ask, no matter what anyone else says or thinks. If you start to have doubts, cancel the doubt and substitute a positive thought instead.
2. Talk to your animal, out loud or mentally, about your training goals. Ask for your animal's opinion and tailor your training program to accommodate your animal's viewpoint. If you have trouble with this step, practice the exercises in chapter 2 for talking with your animal until you feel comfortable talking back and forth.
3. Tell your animal what will be involved and what will be required of him or her. If possible, show your animal another animal doing the desired activity.

4. Make a mental movie of you and your animal performing the activity as if you have already mastered it.

5. While you are engaged in training sessions, comment on what is happening (either in your mind or out loud). If you see your animal is starting to make a mistake, tell her about it right away before she does it. Sometimes the animal can correct the error before it happens.

6. Set up the training situation to be conducive to success. For example, if you are training a dog to come when called, start out in your living room, then build up slowly: do it in the yard on a long line, then in the open in a fenced area, and ultimately out in a field.

7. Offer your animal rewards for doing well. One client told her dressage horse that as soon as he did something correctly, they would end the training session and go visit the donkeys, as that was his favorite thing to do. Once she started offering that reward, she noticed an increase in his ability to do things correctly on the first attempt, and he retained the knowledge from session to session.

8. Give lots of compliments. Animals love compliments as much as we do and they understand them. Just watch for the gleam in your animal's eye when you give a series of compliments. You may also find that with regular compliments, your animal will become much more cooperative during training. If something is going wrong, always assume it is a flaw in your approach, or that your animal is ill or uncomfortable in some way, and set about to find the cause. The first place to start when troubleshooting is to ask the animal, as Neil did with his misbehaving horse.

CHAPTER 6
Dealing with Bad Behaviors

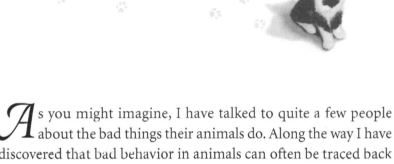

$\mathcal{A}$s you might imagine, I have talked to quite a few people about the bad things their animals do. Along the way I have discovered that bad behavior in animals can often be traced back to something a human did or did not do. If you want to resolve a problem, start by figuring out what created it. You can use intuitive communication to do this by simply asking an animal, "Why are you acting this way?" Often you will discover the basis for the behavior, and you can then set about to change it.

One thing that does not work when dealing with bad behaviors is getting angry, punishing, or blaming. When someone calls me and says, "I want you to tell my animal that he has to shape up or he's history," I try to get the person to calm down and take a more reasoned approach, because if you want to change your animal's bad behavior, you have to be willing to work at it and commit your time and resources. The longer the behavior has been going on, the more effort may be required to resolve it. Your faith that the problem can be resolved and your commitment to do whatever it takes will, most certainly, get you where you want to go.

Animals come into our lives for a reason — even the ones who have behavior problems. We learn from every one of them, either something about ourselves and how to live or something that will be helpful for all our other animals. My now-deceased dog Dougal taught me a lot about dealing with bad behaviors. I met him when I was managing a volunteer creek-restoration project in Oakland, California. We saw him tied up in one of the yards next to the creek where we were working, and occasionally he would escape and come over and visit. One morning a volunteer from the neighborhood called me in a panic because Dougal had gotten loose and chased a child, who had climbed a wall to get away from him. The police had been called and the dog was going to be taken away. The volunteer asked if she could bring him to me to save his life. I agreed.

I called Dougal a chocolate wolfhound because he was clearly a mix of Irish wolfhound and chocolate Labrador. He was also therefore quite large. The problem with him was that he was completely uncivilized. He was an untrained and unneutered male dog who was very hyperactive. He'd had no experience living in a house. For at least six months I tried everything I could think of to find him a new home, meanwhile taking him, in desperation, from one obedience class to another. Then something clicked and he started to calm down. Eventually, after four obedience classes, he turned into the sweetest, gentlest dog I have ever known, and

Dougal

no money would have bought him a new home. Dougal taught me that a good, positive-reinforcement training program[1] is the antidote to a world of bad behaviors. He also taught me that you might not recognize your perfect dog when you first meet him.

WHEN YOU SHOULD CALL A VET
VERSUS A COMMUNICATOR

Sometimes, just talking intuitively with an animal can bring about big changes in behavior, as you will discover from the stories in this chapter. Usually though, intuitive communication is most effective when combined with a training program and holistic health-care practices. And there are a number of situations where it is more appropriate to consult a health-care practitioner rather than an animal communicator. Here are the top ten complaints I get from clients about their animals that I feel fall into this category, with those that occur most often listed first. When people call me with these issues, I refer them to a veterinarian, preferably a holistic veterinarian, or some other holistic health-care practitioner (such as chiropractors, animal massage therapists, and energy healers). Once they have seen a professional health-care practitioner, then they can call me back me for a follow-up intuitive communication session.

1. Inappropriate Urination in Cats

"Inappropriate urination" means when a cat urinates on the rug, outside of the box, on the bed, in the bathtub, on the kitchen stove, in the heating vents, and so on. If my sample of callers is representative, this is a problem that plagues at least half the human race. Inappropriate urination can occur because of a bladder infection, crystals in the urine, or some other problem with the bladder or kidney of the cat. A cat with this behavior must be examined by a veterinarian, as these conditions can be fatal. For my animals, I prefer to work with both a traditional veterinarian (for diagnosis, surgery, and some other services) and a holistic veterinarian (for holistic treatment options).

Often a cat is purposely urinating in the wrong places precisely to tell her person that there is something physically wrong. When people ask me to use intuition to determine whether there is a physical problem, I have to refuse. It's not only ill-advised but illegal for an animal communicator to try to make a medical diagnosis. Intuitive communication is not an exact science; you can be wrong. It is best not to take a chance like that with the health of your animal. To get your cat checked, have a veterinarian test the cat's urine for bacteria, crystals, and specific gravity.[2] If your veterinarian finds physical problems, I would advise you to also consult a holistic veterinarian to decide what to do for treatment.

When inappropriate urination happens only occasionally, and is associated with the person going away for a trip or some other obvious cause, it is more likely to be behavioral-only, which can be addressed through intuitive communication. But even then, the stress of having you leave could cause your cat to develop a bladder infection when you go away on trips. So it is always best to get a checkup. If it turns out not to be a physical problem, then it would be appropriate to talk with the cat, find out what's wrong, and go from there.

2. When Animals Itch, Lick, and Bite Themselves

When cats and dogs have problems licking and biting themselves, it is rarely a psychological problem. I would not say "never" about anything, but usually I send people to holistic veterinarians for this problem, and they typically put such an animal on a real food diet (which includes human-grade meat, either raw or cooked, and organic, lightly cooked vegetables and grains), with herbs for building the immune system, and supplements for improving the digestive health and vigor of the animal. I have heard of this method working in many cases. I know this approach worked with my dog Dougal, who each year developed a staph infection from seasonal allergies and got red rashes all over his body. Before feeding raw food was the thing to do, I decided to put him on a raw diet (which, as the name implies, involves primarily raw meat, raw bones, and vegetables). A lot of people thought I was going to kill my dog by feeding him raw food, and they were waiting for him to keel over. Instead, within four days of starting on raw food, his red bumps were gone, his hair started to grow back, and he stopped itching.

Itching, licking, and biting can also be caused by fleas, but before you reach for a flea collar, you might want to read Dr. Martin Goldstein's book *The Nature of Animal Healing*. After you do, you will probably want to use the more natural ways to control fleas, which are available and work well. I have included information on the raw diet and sources for information on alternative flea control methods in the Resources section (page 181).

3. Refusing to Go Upstairs, Onto the Couch, or Into the Car

At the first sign that your dog or cat is reluctant or refuses to walk up or jump up, ask your holistic veterinarian to evaluate your animal's spine and joints. If the problem turns out to be arthritis or joint stiffness, consider trying chiropractic manipulation, massage, and acupuncture for your animal. These modalities work well for people and are readily available for animals now, too. Holistic veterinarians can also help you with herbs, supplements, and real food diets to address arthritis and other problems with joints and the spine.

4. Horse Bucking or Acting Aggressive

Bad behaviors in horses often have a physical cause, such as sore teeth, sore backs, bad saddles, improper diet, bad bits, and poor foot trimming. Before you decide to send your horse off to boot camp for training, check out how he is feeling physically. You might want to start by having a horse body-worker do a massage. Ask the person to tell you all the areas he or she finds that are painful or problem areas. You could then have a horse chiropractor adjust your horse. See the Resources section (page 181) for more information on natural horse training and holistic options for horses. If you eliminate all the possible physical problems, then it may come down to using communication and training.

5. Dog Eating Rocks and Feces

When people call about a dog who eats rocks or eats its own feces or the feces of other dogs, I refer them to holistic veterinarians, because a normal, healthy dog won't do that. However, dogs will eat every other kind of feces in the world, and that is just normal, disgusting dog behavior: the never-ending search for good stomach bacteria. My clients who have had this problem with their dog tell me that the holistic veterinarians had them switch to a real food diet with digestive supplements, which completely corrected the behavior. When dogs eat rocks or other hard objects, it can become a life-threatening situation that requires surgery, so it is nice to know that people have found a holistic solution.

6. Animal Doesn't Like to Be Touched

Sometimes when an animal doesn't like being touched, it is the result of abuse or lack of exposure to being touched when young, and this can be changed with intuitive communication. But such behavior can also be caused by pain and discomfort. It is always a good idea to have an animal who is exhibiting this behavior checked by a holistic practitioner to make sure the problem is not physical.

7. Cat Meowing and Wandering the House at Night

When cats start meowing and wandering at night, it can be due to undetected disease, pain from arthritis, or senility. My cat Jenny started meowing and being restless at night when she was eighteen. I took her to the veterinary clinic, and they found out that she had hyperthyroidism. She received the radioactive iodine treatment, and her night-prowling behavior ceased until the last year of her life, at twenty-six, when she started it up again. This time it was due to senility. I have also had clients whose cats did this because of arthritis. The best defense for this one is to go to the holistic veterinarian and get your cat checked out.

8. Mares Acting PMS-y

Some mares appear to have hormone imbalances that make them get pretty mean and high-strung during their menstrual cycles. This isn't something you can talk them out of, intuitively or otherwise. Traditional veterinarians often treat this condition with synthetic hormones. I recommend people go to a holistic veterinarian to find a more natural way to balance out their horse's hormones.

9. Losing Hair, Getting Thin, Drinking a Lot

It seems obvious but it needs to be stated: whenever you see your animal losing hair, getting thin, or drinking lots of water, it's time to go to a veterinarian. Those kinds of symptoms can indicate serious health problems and should never be ignored.

10. Horse Won't Stand Still and Cooperate for the Farrier

I would say that well over half of the horses who are difficult when it comes time to trim and shoe them are trying to tell their people that they don't like either the farrier or what the farrier does. My suggestion is to find a really excellent barefoot trimmer for your horse and see if this behavior doesn't improve. Check the Resources section (page 182).

WHEN YOU SHOULD ALSO CALL A TRAINER

Once you have eliminated physical issues as the cause of a bad behavior, you can use intuitive communication to help resolve the problem. However, some bad behaviors can be addressed better through a combination of intuitive communication and animal training techniques. In this section, I have identified the top ten calls that I receive that fall into this category, with the most common calls listed first. When people contact me with one of these problems, I do an intuitive session, and I also refer the person to a professional animal trainer for additional help.

I recommend working only with trainers who use nonviolent methods. This may require careful research and selection on your part. You can immediately eliminate any dog trainer who proposes the use of alpha rolls, prong collars, hanging a dog from his leash and collar, ear pinching, hitting, or electroshock collars. Also avoid any horse trainer who hits, ties up, or restrains the horse, or uses whips, harsh spurs, harsh bits, or anything else that hurts or scares the horse. Keep in mind that even if the training method you choose is nonviolent, the trainer might not be. When you work with a trainer, if something doesn't feel right to you, and your animal seems stressed out and unhappy, look for a new trainer. Keep searching until it feels right; that's when you will know you have the right combination of method and trainer.

1. Aggression

Aggression is a big problem in all animals. Cats, dogs, and horses may attack, slash, or bite other cats, dogs, horses, and humans, even their own people. If you have this problem and you have eliminated the possibility that the animal is acting aggressively because of pain or discomfort, then you will probably have to include training as part of the method for resolving the problem. Aggression must be addressed immediately, as an aggressive animal can be dangerous to both humans and other animals.

2. Separation Anxiety

Separation anxiety is the name given to a range of behaviors exhibited when an animal has fear about being left alone, such as when a dog is left at home during the day, or a horse is separated from the herd. As far as I can tell, cats don't typically get separation anxiety, though a few can. Cats can, however, get pretty ticked off that you had the audacity to desert them and go on a silly vacation, and they can act out as a consequence.

There are good training guides for dealing with this problem in dogs (some of which I list in the Resources section, page 183). I haven't found much written about how to address this in horses, but you can use similar techniques. For example, a desensitization technique used for dogs involves getting a dog accustomed to being separated a little bit at a time. For a horse you could start by taking the horse for a short walk, still in sight of the herd and giving lots of great treats. You would do that every day, increasing the length of the walk and eventually going out of sight of the herd. The horse should be able to adjust and let go of her anxiety as you extend the separation. In addition to the training program, intuitive communication can really help any animal, including a cat, who has separation anxiety.

3. Dog Who Isn't Housebroken

Dogs are creatures of habit. To get them to stop peeing in the house, you have to recondition them to pee elsewhere, so you will need to use some training techniques along with communication.

4. Dog Who Won't Come When Called

As with a dog who isn't housebroken, dealing with a dog who won't come to you when called is a training issue. Great treats and a consistent, graduated training program help to create a perfect recall.

5. Dog Who Barks

Barking is often caused by lack of exercise. If you have a barking dog, find a positive-reinforcement training class and sign up. Also take your dog for regular walks. Find out what stimuli make your dog bark and work to reduce your dog's exposure to those stimuli. Intuitive communication can also help.

6. Dog Who Digs

Dogs love to dig. Rather than trying to stop this behavior, you can persuade your dog, through nonviolent training and intuitive communication, to dig politely in one specified area.

7. Horse Who Spooks or Won't Trailer Well

Natural horsemanship training techniques, combined with bodywork, herbs, flower essences, and holistic care and feeding, will usually resolve the problem of a horse that spooks or won't trailer well. Intuitive communication also helps.

8. Dog Who Bolts Out the Door or Runs Away

Running out the door is a training problem if ever there was one. Running away is more complex. Training will help resolve it, but you also need a good fence, and your dog needs to have a good life — otherwise, he may just keep sending you the message that he isn't happy until you finally get it. Communicating with your dog intuitively is important, but so is taking him for a great walk every day, or taking him with you to the café for a cappuccino.

9. Dog Who Chases and/or Kills Cats

Dogs can be trained to be nice to cats. I have even had clients who used training and communication to get their dogs to stop killing cats.

10. Dog Who Jumps on People

Dogs who jump on people can easily be trained to cease and desist using nonviolent training techniques.

USING INTUITIVE COMMUNICATION
TO IDENTIFY THE PROBLEM

The first step in using intuition to correct bad behavior is to interview your animal to find out what is causing the behavior and what the animal needs in order to change.

EXERCISE
Interview Your Animal

It can be hard to ask your animal about an issue that is emotionally charged for you, but you can do it and get helpful results. People worry that they are making things up when they record what they think they are receiving from their animals. That is an unavoidable situation. The only way to deal with it is to follow your feelings. Keep asking yourself how you feel as you ask your animal questions, and write down your impressions. In my experience, if you do this, you will probably get accurate information about the cause of the behavior problem your animal is experiencing.

Find a quiet time with no distractions and create a list of questions you have for your animal regarding a specific behavior problem. Here are some possible questions to start with:

- Why are you acting this way?
- Are you reflecting something in me?
- What do you need from me?
- What do you need to change the behavior?
- If I do [suggest a specific remedy], will it help?
- Do you want to change and resolve this problem?
- Will you help me find the ways to do that?

Add any other questions that are specific to your situation. Now have an intuitive dialogue with your animal. Ask your first question and then wait for a response. Take the questions one at a time; do not go on to the next question until you have recorded whatever impression comes in. You may only get a vague feeling, and that's fine. If you can't sense any impressions, make a guess about how your animal would answer the question. Whether you feel confident in the responses you receive or not, assume that they accurately reflect your animal's thoughts and feelings. Then, based on what your animal tells you, design a behavior modification program using the components described in the rest of this chapter to deal with the problem.

Is Your Animal Mirroring You?

Animals can mimic, or mirror, us physically and emotionally. Our animals are so close to us that it is natural for them to get in sync with us in this way. If we are happy and healthy, then this is not a problem! But it is not uncommon for a veterinarian to treat an animal for the same illness or injury that the owner has. This can happen with emotions and beliefs, too. Before I realized what I was doing, I used to make my dog Brydie fearful of other dogs because of my fear of how she would interact with them. Once I changed my negative expectation and got rid of my fear, she became a normal, happy, dog-loving dog. Step back and take an objective look at yourself and at your animal's bad behavior: Do you have the same problem your animal does, or might you be causing the problem because of your feelings and beliefs? By reflecting our imbalances through mirroring, our animals help us to heal.

If you suspect your animal is mirroring, the best way to deal with it is to correct the problem in yourself. For example, if you have a bad back and your animal does, too, find new solutions to your back problem. Or, if you have issues about abandonment and your animal does, too, address the problem in yourself first. Correcting the problem in yourself can sometimes be all that is needed to clear it in your animal.

Also have a talk with your animal about the situation. Explain that while you love the fact that your animal is very close to you, it would be best for you if she could be a model of good health and happy behavior for you to follow, rather than reflecting something that is out of balance for you. Tell her thanks for showing you the issue and ask if she can now let it go. Promise that you will work to resolve the problem in yourself. Also implement whatever remedies are appropriate for correcting the problem for your animal.

Reassure and Redirect Your Animal

Once you have your animal's input about a problem, and you are pretty sure your animal is not mirroring you, have a talk with your animal and tell her how you feel about what you have learned. For example, if your animal is shy, you could tell her how much you love her and want her to feel comfortable. Explain what you will do to keep her safe so that she can feel more confident. If she said she was worried about other animals attacking her, you can promise her you will control the other animals so that won't happen.

Use intuitive communication to give your animal instructions about what you want and why you don't like what she is doing. Sometimes, just talking to your animal in detail about the issue can have a positive impact.

EXPAND THE COACH APPROACH

When you are working with a behavior problem with your animal, take the Coach Approach that I describe in chapter 5 and expand it with one or more of the following techniques: Time-Out, Shift or Consequences, New Job, and New Name. Any or all of them may help with your particular problem.

Remember, you may want to include a number of other components to help change a behavior problem, such as training and holistic remedies. As you develop and begin your behavior modification program, write in your notebook daily to track the changes that may be occurring in response to what you are doing.

To review, here are the steps to the Coach Approach:

- Believe that your animal can change for the better.
- Cancel negative thoughts about your animal, substitute positive ones, and visualize the best outcome to the situation.

- Tell your animal what you want to change and how you are going to go about it. Get feedback and adjust your program accordingly.
- Show your animal your dream of how she can be (make mental movies).
- Give rewards and compliments for the slightest improvement you observe.

EXERCISE
Give a Time-Out

If your animal backslides after showing some signs of improvement, try taking him aside and telling him how you feel about his error. Explain how excited you were that there was progress, and how disappointed you are with the error. Suggest ways that your animal can avoid making the same mistake again. After your talk, give your animal a few minutes' time-out (in a separate room or fenced area) with the instruction to think about what happened and how to change it in the future.

EXERCISE
Shift or Consequences

This technique is exactly what its name says, and it has three simple steps:

1. Tell and show your animal, using mental movies, what you want changed. Make sure as you create the movie in your head that you also feel the things you are imagining as if you were experiencing them in real life.
2. Tell and show your animal the consequences if the behavior doesn't change.

3. Then tell and show your animal what you want again. This time include all the great things that will happen if the behavior shifts.

EXERCISE
Assign a New Job

Take the bad behavior you are trying to change and treat it like a really poor job description that needs to be revised. For example, a cat spraying the walls might think he is performing a necessary duty: spraying the walls to make the house smell like him so that other cats won't come around. Change that job description so that it works for you and the cat. In this case, you might change it to something like: spraying outside of the house so that cats in the area know to stay away, while keeping the house clean. Here are some other possibilities: for a dog, change chasing cats to becoming the protector of the cats in the house. Or, change the job of digging up the yard to one of helping keep the plants nice while digging in a special place just for dogs in order to help mix the soil there. Once you have designed your new job description, explain it to your animal, and then visualize your animal doing the new job you have identified.

Another approach is to think of some new jobs your animal can do for you. This is especially helpful if the bad behavior you are dealing with is due to a lack of activity or excitement in the animal's life. New jobs can be anything you think your animal might like doing. I ask my cats to help me write, and I ask my horses to help me find people to ride with. If you assign new jobs, keep track of what you have assigned. Write it down and post it on the refrigerator. Then track how your animal is doing with the new job and make sure to give ongoing feedback.

Here is the process for evaluating and changing your animal's job description.

- Ask your animal what jobs he or she is doing for you now. Record whatever impressions you get about this in response. If nothing comes in, make your best guess about what jobs your animal thinks he or she is doing currently.
- Ask what job your animal might like to do. Record your results.
- Explain what job you would like your animal to do for you. This could be revising a job the animal currently does (like digging in the garden) or it could be a new job. A job can be something very straightforward, like protecting the yard or making you exercise, or something more refined, like helping you find the right path in life, or helping educate your other animals.
- Ask your animal if he or she likes the new job(s) you have proposed. Record your impressions, or make your best guess about how your animal feels about these jobs.
- Assign whichever new jobs you feel your animal would like to do. Relieve your animal of any old jobs your animal no longer wants to do.
- Write down the new jobs and keep track of how your animal is doing at the new jobs.
- Praise your animal for how he or she is doing at the new jobs.

EXERCISE
Assign a New Name

If you think your animal's name could be part of the problem, then try changing it for two weeks and see what happens. Changing an animal's name can completely change the animal's personality and eliminate behavioral problems. Perhaps you never liked your animal's name, or your animal's current name doesn't have the right ring to it; you may not be the only one who feels this way. I have seen an animal change overnight once they have a name that is right for them.

If you decide to try this, first ask your animal if he or she likes the current name. If you get the sense the animal likes the current name, then don't try to change it unless you really hate it. If you really hate the current name, and it is a name that came with the animal, talk to your animal and see if you can't negotiate a name change. If you get the sense your animal does not like the current name, start researching new names. Make a list of the names that you like that reflect who you want and believe your animal can be. Then ask your animal about the new names. Try out whichever one he or she likes and see what happens.

SUGGESTIONS FOR SPECIFIC CASES

Here are some more specific suggestions of intuitive techniques for some of the more common behavioral problems I deal with. Use these suggestions along with the expanded Coach Approach I described above.

Talking with Aggressive Animals

As I said earlier, aggression in animals could be life-threatening and must be addressed immediately by a combination of restraint, positive training, and holistic remedies. You can also add intuitive communication and the Coach Approach to that. Here are some additional suggestions for resolving your animal's aggressive behavior. If your animal is aggressive because of past trauma, talk to him about your feelings about what he went through and give him your best advice about how he should deal with his past.

Dogs

If your dog is aggressive to other dogs, tell him that from now on you will protect him. He doesn't have to take the lead anymore because you will. Make sure he is always safe by keeping him away from overly aggressive animals. If your dog is aggressive to people, explain that such aggression would only be appropriate if someone were physically trying to harm you. Tell him that otherwise you would like him to just be neutral to people. Try using the Shift or Consequences, New Job, and even New Name techniques for your dog.

Horses

If you have a horse who is overly aggressive to you, explain to her that you will be using a variety of methods to address the problem and that the behavior can't go on. Make sure to use the Coach Approach and include the Shift or Consequences technique when you communicate with her. Positive natural horsemanship training will be essential to reversing this problem. You will also need to thoroughly investigate whether she is having pain or discomfort in any way. If your horse is overly aggressive to other horses, use the Coach Approach and the Shift or Consequences technique. You can also ask the other horses or any other animals who know your horse for help in getting your horse to change her behavior. Just talk to them intuitively, explain the problem, and ask for their help.

Cats

For cats who tend to bite and scratch their people, I have found the following combination of vocalization and intuitive communication helpful. Using the Coach Approach, explain to your cat that the attacks have to stop and explain why you don't like being attacked. Tell your cat you will be making an awful noise whenever she decides to bite or scratch, but if she refrains from doing that you won't make the awful noise. The next time she starts to attack, immediately scream, "Ah, ah!" at the top of your lungs like a drill sergeant. The hoped-for response will be disdain and disgust on the part of your cat. Do it again the next time she tries to attack. If you get the volume and the timing right, you should only have to do a big correction a few times. After that you will probably only have to say, "Ah, remember our agreement," in a normal tone of voice, in order to extinguish any thought your cat may have of attacking you.

Cow 553

Sometimes, communicating intuitively with an animal about aggressive behavior can turn things around immediately, as in this extraordinary story from Marie Rubin, a student in one of my advanced classes. At the time, Marie's daughter was in college and doing an internship at a black Angus breeding farm. The cows at the farm wore numbered ear tags so that the farmer could tell them apart. Marie's daughter called to ask her to communicate intuitively with a female cow, number 553, who was the herd boss and very aggressive about protecting her new calf. Everyone was terrified of cow 553, and when they had to go near her, they stayed close to the fence for a fast getaway, trying to put other cows in between to avoid getting charged.

In my advanced class, Marie had learned how to talk intuitively from a distance with an animal she had never seen, without using a picture. Marie said that when she sat down to do this with 553, she had every intention of reading the cow the riot act and ordering her to leave her daughter alone. But when she introduced herself mentally to the cow, Marie got a sense of calm and cooperation. She and the cow were just two mothers comparing notes and protecting their young. It made no difference that they were different species. Marie complimented 553 on her handsome calf, and expressed her admiration for the way she took such good care of him. Marie felt the cow was pleased, and then she heard the cow mentally ask her about her own offspring. Marie sent 553 a mental image of her daughter — and she explained that she was very concerned because some of the cows were threatening the students, and Marie couldn't be there to protect her daughter. Marie did not directly tell 553 that she was the one scaring everyone. Then she sent 553 a mental image of herself running at a cow, and knocking her off her feet, to show 553 how she would protect her daughter. The cow seemed impressed, and mentally sent a promise to Marie that she would not let any cow threaten her daughter. Marie thanked 553 for her help.

The next morning Marie's daughter called to say that when she and another intern went into the pens, all the cows backed away from them. At first, the interns were terrified because they had no buffers, and there was nowhere to hide. However, cow 553 just stood in the center of the pen watching over them and keeping them safe. Neither 553 nor any other cow ever bothered Marie's daughter again. Marie reconnected with the cow several times to express her gratitude.

Calming an Animal Who Has Separation Anxiety

Whether it is a horse or a dog, one of the best ways to address separation anxiety behavior is to tell the animal where you are going and how long you will be gone. Horses tend to get anxious when they have to leave their friends. In dogs, the syndrome occurs when they have to stay at home and be separated from their people. Whenever you have to leave your animals in the house, explain what time you will be back, and why your animal can't come along. Cats appreciate this, too; even though, as I said, they don't appear to get anxious the way dogs do, they can get upset about your leaving. Reassure a nervous animal that you will be checking in intuitively with him during the day. While you are out and when you have a chance, find a quiet place to close your eyes and tune in to your animal. Imagine him in front of you, say hello, mentally or out loud, and tell him how you're doing and when you will be home. Imagine him being calm and resting, and send him a feeling of love. Talking to animals with separation anxiety can really help when done in combination with other remedies listed in the Resources section (page 181).

Redirecting Inappropriate Urination in Cats

Once you are sure inappropriate urination does not have a physical cause, you can use communication to find out what is bothering your cat. If your cat is urinating as a way to stake out territory, discuss that and offer alternatives, like changing the job description, so the marking is all done outside of the house. If the problem is that the cats within your household are not getting along, go back to chapter 4 for ideas for creating peace within your home. If you feel your cat is resentful or angry with you for some reason, discuss the situation in detail with your cat. Offer compromises and suggest all the ways you can think of for resolving the issue.

One thing to consider for cats who are indoor-only is to provide some kind of safe outside space. One of the best ways to do this is by setting up a cat fencing system to give them safe access to a yard. This can help extinguish urination problems overnight. If you decide to do cat fencing, tell your cat that in exchange for this nice thing you are doing, you would like him to stop peeing in the house. See the Resources section (page 184) for more on cat fencing and other ideas.

Housebreaking a Dog

As with cats, make sure your dog's urination problems don't have a physical cause. Then use the Coach Approach and a good positive training program to housebreak a dog of any age, even one who has had a long-standing problem.

Achieving Perfect Recall

Use the Coach Approach and the techniques described on the video *Really Reliable Recall* (see the Resources section, page 183) to create a perfect recall behavior in your dog.

Putting an End to Barking

If the barking dog is your own, there are many good training guides for how to stop the barking. You can also talk intuitively to your dog about the barking (as in the story about Buster that follows).

If the barking dog belongs to a neighbor, it gets more complicated. In that case, talk to the barking dog intuitively to explain why you hate the barking and would like it to stop. Then tell the dog that you will give her a reward if she can curb her barking. Pick whatever reward seems best: a healthy treat, regularly patting and talking with her, sending love, having a talk with her owner about taking her for more walks, and so on. Make sure to follow through on your promise. Also visualize the dog being quiet, calm, and content. You could also imagine her having a better life and tell her to imagine this for herself as well. These techniques have worked for a number of people I know.

Buster

Here is how Rebecca Trono got her dog Buster to stop barking. Rebecca and her husband had invited some guests to dinner. During the week before the dinner, Rebecca had a series of intuitive talks with Buster, to prepare him for the guests' arrival, which would typically set off lots of barking from Buster. She began her sessions by sending Buster visualizations of the guests coming in, complete with detailed pictures of each person, including their names. She showed him that it would be a wonderful, happy thing to have the guests in their home, explaining to Buster that they would be there to have fun and to have dinner. She told him they were not going to harm anyone, so barking would not be appropriate. She gave him permission to give a couple of alert barks, to signal that the guests had arrived, but once the guests entered the door, Buster was to be quiet. Then she visualized hugs all around, smiles, and relaxed attitudes, and sent Buster a feeling of love and pride in his ability to refrain from barking at her friends. She told her husband what she was doing with Buster, and he gave a hearty laugh and said, "Good luck!" The evening of the dinner came and the guests arrived. Buster jumped up, walked out to the mudroom, greeted the people, whom he had never met, with a casual, uninterested sniff, and then returned to the living room. He didn't even bark once! Her husband said that if he had not been there to witness Buster's behavior himself, he never would have believed it in a million years.

After that, Rebecca and Buster came to an agreement: He could bark a couple of short barks if someone came to the door, but if someone just walked by, he couldn't bark. He was allowed to grumble as much as he liked but not growl. She sent him pictures of his compliance, barking when someone was at the door, and being quiet when people just passed by. Every time he stuck with their deal, she went crazy with praise, and sent him lots of love and intense pride. She also sent visualizations of him not sticking with the deal and her feelings of disappointment and sadness. Amazingly, within days, she noticed that Buster was sticking with the agreement. Now, if he slips up every so often, all she has to do is say, "Uh-oh, Buster, remember our deal," and he immediately stops barking.

Rebecca and her dogs, Emmett (left) and Buster

Digging

Use the Coach Approach and New Job technique to redefine digging for your animal. Make it something useful to be done in certain areas that you identify. Explain that you really need your animal to dig in those specific areas. Show her pictures of the rest of the yard hole-free. Redirect digging away from where you don't want it, bury a bone or something she wants to direct her to dig where you want, and then praise her enormously for digging where she is supposed to.

Running Away

Use the Coach Approach to find out why your animal is running away. Then devise a management program to deal with the problem. Incorporate a fun, positive training class into the program.

Trailering Reluctant Horses

Try these intuitive methods for a horse who is afraid to go into a trailer. Explain where you are going, how long you will be there, and what you will be doing. Make whatever promises are applicable about the trip. For example, if you will be coming home right after the horse show, promise that. Also promise to drive slowly and carefully. Then offer a treat and gently encourage the horse to enter the trailer. Tell him he can take his time. Breathe and get relaxed yourself. If he gets on, give him the treat, and have another ready to lead him farther in. If he is willing, tie him in, but if he wants to back out, let him do that so he knows he is not trapped. To encourage him to go in, someone could stand behind swinging a rope in a gentle circle; the horse will naturally move away from the rope and toward the trailer. Also use the mental movies outlined in the Coach Approach.

Spooking, Bucking, and Rearing

All of these behaviors could be physically based. Make sure to check that first. Then use positive training and the Coach Approach to address the problems.

Teaching Tolerance to Touch

If you have an animal who does not like to be touched, find out what bad experiences he may have had in the past and assure him you will prevent anything like that from happening again. Talk to your animal about why you like to cuddle and pat. Tell him that each week you would like to pat a new area and pat a bit longer. Ask if he would be willing to do that for you. Then go very slowly to extend your patting sessions and give lots of praise and thanks as you go along. Only do what your animal is willing to accept.

Dealing with a Cat-Aggressive Dog

If a dog really is a cat killer, it will be hard to reform her. I have one client who was able to do that, but not without losing a few more cats in the process. If your dog is just aggressive to cats, then you can use the Coach Approach, training, and holistic remedies to address the problem. Make sure to control your dog with a leash and soft muzzle until and unless you are sure you are not dealing with a dog who will kill your cats.

Jasmine

Pamela Ginger Flood, who works as a professional animal communicator, was able to reform a rescue dog who was cat-aggressive through a combination of training and intuitive communication. Jasmine, a German shepherd–Rottweiler mix, was to be euthanized at the local shelter. A shelter volunteer called Pamela asking if she could foster Jasmine to save her life. Pamela took her in and after six months of good, natural food, gentle exercise, and herbs, Jasmine was a healthy new dog. However, there was one problem: Jasmine was very cat-aggressive and Pamela had two cats. Jasmine was grateful for being rescued and desperately wanted to stay with Pamela. So, using intuitive communication, Pamela made a deal with her: Jasmine could stay as long as she completely ignored the cats. Any aggressive behavior toward the cats would be a deal breaker. Jasmine agreed. At first she would "alert" at the presence of a cat, but a curt "Jasmine!" and she would immediately lie down and put her head on the floor. The cats soon learned that Jasmine was not allowed to try to eat them, and they got very bold. They would walk up to within an inch of the dog's nose and flip their tails at her. Jasmine's eyes would get very big and she would look pleadingly at Pamela, but she would not move. About six months later, Pamela adopted another cat. Jasmine's first response was, "This one doesn't count, right?" Pamela assured her that this cat did, indeed, count, and Jasmine gave a great sigh and left the new cat alone. She has never chased another cat.

CONSULTING AN ANIMAL COMMUNICATOR

If you have tried everything and nothing is working, or if you just want some professional insight into your animal's behavior problem, you can consult a professional animal communicator. If you decide to do that, take your time to select someone who a friend recommends, or someone with a good record of success in solving behavior problems.

The Story of a Reformed Laundry Stealer

This is a story about using intuitive communication to correct a rather unusual bad behavior: laundry stealing. Anna Patient called me to consult with her cat Bushra, who had taken to stealing laundry from the neighbors. Anna said Bushra's bad habit started right

Bushra

after they moved to a new place. Bushra began to take clothes out of the washing machine in the basement and strew them around the apartment. The first time it happened, Anna was away for the weekend and a neighbor was looking after the cats. Anna was mortified when she came home to discover that there was a bra under the dining room table, and knickers up and down the stairs to the cellar. It took her a while to figure out what had happened, and some further explanation to convince the neighbor that the cat had done it!

The problem escalated when Anna moved again, to a ground-floor apartment in a more rural area. In nice weather people hung out their clothes to dry, and Bushra brought back all sorts of things. By the end of the summer, Anna would have a bag full of odd socks, boxers, knickers, rags, and gardening gloves. The largest items Bushra brought back were a towel and a T-shirt. All would have been well except that one set of neighbors became unpleasant. They began to deliberately leave clothing out with their name included so that Anna would know it was theirs. They gave Anna an ultimatum: either stop Bushra or she goes. Anna called me at that point, and I talked to Bushra, explaining the situation and what was needed of her. Anna said Bushra stopped taking things from the neighbors after that talk. Anna followed up as I instructed, by visualizing Bushra always walking right past the house of the nasty neighbors. Anna also put out socks every day in the garden for Bushra to collect, as Bushra had indicated she wanted to continue to find and bring home her treasures. She said Bushra seemed content with this as long as she washed the socks regularly, since Bushra had a preference for just-washed laundry.

CHAPTER 7
Aiding an Animal in Distress

*T*he stories in this chapter are from people who are no different than you. They learned to communicate intuitively just as you can, and they used their skill to help animals at shelters or in crisis situations. As you read, you will learn how it is done and discover the miracles that are possible through connecting intuitively. Here are two stories from a former student, Kate Wilcox, who now practices as a professional animal communicator. Kate traveled to Biloxi, Mississippi, after Hurricane Katrina to help with the animal rescue effort there.

KATRINA RESCUE STORIES

Kate arrived two months after Hurricane Katrina hit the U.S. Gulf Coast. The rescue group she was working with was setting traps to try to recover the thousands of animals made homeless by Katrina. On the east side of Biloxi, a female dog was caught in one of the traps, and she was so agitated that Kate knew she had to go there to help her. The animal control officers thought the dog was just wild, starving, and traumatized from the hurricane, but Kate felt intuitively that something else was going on. The dog was salivating, snarling, and ripping at the trap to get out. Kate checked in with the dog intuitively and told her she knew that the dog needed to get out, and that she would help her. She slipped a leash over the dog's neck and let her out. Kate and a veterinary technician in the group checked the dog for injuries and found none. Then Kate got a strong feeling that the dog had puppies somewhere. The veterinary technician disagreed, saying that the dog's teats were dried up and there were no physical signs of pregnancy, but Kate felt certain the dog had puppies. She told the dog intuitively to go find her babies.

The dog took off, towing Kate through blackberry bushes, inside broken-down cars, under piles of rubble, and through brush where Kate had to crawl on her stomach. Kate knew the dog was trying to lose her, but she just kept on asking her to go to the puppies and saying that she would help them. Finally, the dog took her to a house that had been knocked off its foundation. The dog circled the house several times, and then Kate knew that the puppies were under the house.

The veterinary technician who was with her put the dog in a crate, and Kate circled the house again, listening. She heard something coming from the farthest corner of the house. She was afraid to crawl under the house, as it was barely standing, but she got on her stomach and slithered under anyway. Her nose kept bumping on the floor joists, so she had to wriggle on her belly with her head to the side. Dirt was spilling into her shirt and pants. But she knew the puppies were there because she could now hear their

Kate and Mama Dog

cries clearly. She found her way to their den. The mama dog had dug a hole, and in it there were eight puppies who were about three hours old. Kate managed to turn over and unbutton her flannel shirt. She put the puppies on her stomach, buttoned them in, and slid back out from under the house on her back. When she returned the puppies to their mother, the dog looked at Kate with such intense trust and gratitude that it made Kate cry and get goose bumps at the same time.

In another rescue effort, Kate worked with a team of people consisting of a veterinary technician from Washington, two animal control officers from Boston, several animal rescue people from the area, and two photojournalists, all of whom thought of Kate as the freak from California who claimed to communicate with animals. The team was trapping abandoned dogs who were running in packs in the streets of Biloxi. One such pack had moved into several houses in East Biloxi, and the residents who were returning to the area could not get back inside their homes because of the dogs. The group had been trying for three days to trap this particular pack of dogs with live traps and bait. Most of the dogs had injuries, such as broken legs, open sores, lacerations, and fight wounds.

Kate and one of the puppies

The team managed to get all but one little dog, a Scottie mix, who was very fast and who trusted no one. His eyelids were bleeding, and he had a large laceration from his chest to his stomach. The animal control officers had tried to catch him with the poles with no luck. The dog would not go near the traps despite the steaks left for bait. He was in a stressed state because the rest of his pack had been taken to the shelter, and he was now alone.

Kate walked over to a vacant lot next to the house where he was hiding and sat down on the grass. She spoke to him intuitively, explaining that she wished him no harm, and that if he would come to her, she would take care of him. She also told him that his pack family was at the shelter, and it would be very hard for him to survive alone. He poked his head out from under the house

Toto

where he was hiding. Then, to the amazement of everyone watching, he slowly walked over to where Kate was sitting. Kate opened her arms to him, and the dog crawled into her lap. She held him close and intuitively wrapped her heart around him. The animal control officers ran up and wanted to crate the dog, but he would not have it. He knew Kate was a safe person and he was sticking with her. Kate opened her truck door

and the dog hopped in. He sat in the middle of the seat on the console and would not take his eyes off Kate. She took him to the shelter, where his wounds were tended to. No one came to claim him, so Kate did. She named him Toto. They aren't in Biloxi anymore, and he is the love of her life.

HELPING RESCUE-ANIMALS

There are many ways to assist shelter or other rescued animals using intuitive communication. You can help an animal understand what is happening to him and why he is being rescued. You can counsel him and help him deal with his situation emotionally, and you can explain to him what he needs to do to get a good home. When you work with shelter and rescue animals, you use the techniques for connecting and talking with animals you don't know that were introduced in chapter 4. At the end of this chapter I give you a few more tips for doing this. The following stories are some examples of how people have assisted shelter and rescue animals just by talking with them intuitively.

After reading my how-to book, Nathalie Haylar decided to try talking to the animals at the local shelter where she volunteered each weekend. She said she used my techniques on every single dog at the shelter. At one point, one of the workers ran up to her in distress because Nathalie was patting two dogs considered to be aggressive and dangerous. The worker was surprised to see the dogs acting like puppies with her. As soon as the dogs saw the worker, they started barking and showing their teeth. It got scary, but then the female dog came back to Nathalie and leaned against her to be patted. The worker went to the office to get the shelter directors to come see what was happening. All of the shelter staff were amazed, and they asked Nathalie how she had won the dogs' confidence. Nathalie said she simply told the dogs they were beautiful and that she would be delighted if they would let her give them treats and spend time with them. For a while the staff doubted Nathalie, but then they decided they should all try talking to dogs, too.

Skyler

Rebecca Trono also works with her local animal shelter. Rebecca is an energy healer[1] and has added intuitive communication to the skills she uses to help animals. One day a behaviorist at the shelter asked Rebecca to spend some time with a small, white puppy named Skyler. He was about eight months old and had been given up by his owners, a retired couple, because of his incessant guarding and biting behavior. It had gotten to the point where Skyler would guard anything, including discarded tissues he found on the floor, with real, painful bites. The couple felt unable to handle this problem that they may have inadvertently created, and so had regretfully brought Skyler to the shelter.

When Rebecca met with Skyler, he tore around the room while she sat on a dog bed on the floor and conducted an energy healing session in the hopes of calming him down. She watched him without letting him know, keeping her eyes nearly closed and acting uninterested. He tried everything to engage her, including bringing a rubber toy to her and putting it in her lap. Rebecca knew he was baiting her, and that she would be soundly bitten if she tried to pick up the toy, so she ignored it.

After a few minutes, she began communicating with him. She introduced herself and told him the behaviorist had asked her to talk with him. She asked him if he understood why he was now living at the shelter. Rebecca didn't get anything back from Skyler, who continued to run around the room, looking out all the windows. She went on to explain that his biting behaviors had put him there, and that the staff was concerned for him. No response. She then said, "Skyler, you *must* stop biting people. If you do not stop, the staff will have to put you to sleep." Immediately she heard the words, "So what?" and received the impression that he was totally unconcerned. She replied, "No, you don't understand. I'm saying that if you do not stop biting people and guarding things, they will have to kill you, Skyler. They will end your physical incarnation. You will be sent back to start over again." While she didn't receive words in response to this statement, she did feel thoughtfulness, as though Skyler was really taking in the information and understanding it. She finished the energy healing session and closed the communication, thanking Skyler for giving her the opportunity to spend some time with him, and saying she hoped he would make some positive changes for himself.

She returned to the shelter two weeks later and saw the behaviorist who had requested she speak with Skyler. She asked how Skyler was doing and the behaviorist replied, "His attitude changed almost immediately after you talked with him. He responded to training very well, and we were actually able to place him in a new home."

Kyle and Tiffany

Through her work with the shelter animals, Rebecca was also able to help a pair of cats who just weren't getting adopted, and no one could figure out why.

Kyle and Tiffany had been at the shelter for about five months.

The staff remarked many times that they were surprised at the cats' long stay, because even though they were a bonded pair who had to be adopted together, they were such great cats that everyone felt they should have been scooped up already. Kyle and Tiffany were in a large, wire cage in the lobby, right behind the registration desk. They were the first animals that visitors saw when they entered the shelter, and they had become the staff favorites.

One day, after Rebecca had worked her way through the shelter giving energy healing to most of the animals, she came to Kyle and Tiffany's cage. She offered them energy healing and began to send it, just enjoying the quiet and calm of the moment. At the time, Rebecca was just starting out as a communicator and did not have a lot of experience or confidence. But just to try it out, she struck up an intuitive conversation with the cats, expecting nothing in return. She explained to them that the staff was concerned about their long stay at the shelter. She told them the shelter's mission was to match them with their "forever home" so they could move on. Suddenly she "heard" a lovely female voice with a British accent say with alarm, "Do you mean *leave*, dear?" Rebecca paused, thinking that either she hadn't *really* just heard that or she was making things up. But she thought she may as well go along with it because she might actually be communicating with the cats.

So Rebecca replied, "Yes, the idea is that you leave." She then heard, "But why would we want to do *that*, dear? We're *famous!*" She was startled at the word "famous," but decided to keep going, all the while thinking to herself, "I can't believe this is happening!"

She explained the staff's mission again, and said they were hoping to find a lovely home for Kyle and Tiffany. Tiffany responded, "But why would we want to go to a home where we would be left alone all day? Here we get so much attention, everyone loves us, we are the first cats people see as they come in, and besides, we're *famous!*"

Rebecca told the cats about the possibility of a wonderful, re-tired person adopting them, one who would make comfy window seats for them, cook chicken livers for treats, and brush, pat, and love them all day long. She asked the cats what they thought of that. It was then that she heard a very low, clearly male voice chime in, "Oh, well, yes, that does sound good!" She went on to tell them that they could send out their desires for that kind of home to the universe and it would be delivered to them. But the catch was that they had to ask for it themselves.

Rebecca then heard Tiffany say, "Yes, I suppose we could think about that, discuss it a bit." Kyle was in agreement, saying, "We will discuss it, and let you know what we think when you come again."

Rebecca thanked them both, closed the energy healing session, and found the volunteer coordinator, with whom she'd had most of her dealings. Rebecca explained what had happened with Kyle and Tiffany, prefaced by the disclaimer that she didn't know if the conversation was "real" or not. Then she asked the coordinator what Tiffany might have meant when she kept saying she and Kyle were famous. "Oh!" the coordinator replied, "Kyle and Tiffany were profiled in our local paper recently. There was a two-page spread complete with photographs of them. So she's right, they *are* famous!"

A week later Rebecca returned to the shelter to find Kyle and Tiffany had been moved to a "kitty bungalow," a little room with glass walls, which gave them lots of room to roam around. She sat down to begin the energy healing session while they moved about. She closed her eyes, began her meditation, and started the energy flowing. She had very little expectation of any communication, but just relaxed and then sent out questions. "So, have you two come to a decision about whether you're ready to leave the shel-ter?" she asked. She got no reply and just stayed with the quiet for a moment, until she got a weird feeling. She opened her eyes and directly in front of her, the two cats were lying on the floor, star-ing up at her intensely. For some reason she had the thought, "Oh, okay, so I guess this is the last time I'll be seeing you two." A week later a retired woman came into the shelter and adopted Kyle and Tiffany.

Murphy

Pamela Ginger Flood, another student turned professional, uses her communication skills to assist the Give a Dog a Bone Foundation[2] in San Francisco, which is dedicated to helping enrich the lives of shelter animals and animals caught in the legal system. They called Pamela to help with an English bulldog named Murphy who had been brought in on a cruelty/neglect seizure case. Murphy was an older dog with health problems; he was in poor physical condition and was acting depressed.

When Pamela communicated with him, he told her that people would walk by his cage and remark on how ugly he was. He added that he thought if he had a red bandana, it might just help. Pamela told the director of the foundation, Corinne Dowling, what Murphy had said. Corinne bought Murphy a red bandana and convinced people to stop making comments around him. Murphy perked up immediately and wouldn't go anywhere without the bandana that made him so handsome! Murphy became one of the first two dogs ever allowed to be fostered during a court process. This was a major victory for the foundation, as previously all the dogs in court cases were kept in very small cages for months on end.

HELPING ANIMALS MANIFEST A BETTER LIFE

I have found that it is possible to help animals in a bad situation use their own intention to create a better future for themselves. As we saw in chapter 1, researchers are finding that there is real science behind the idea that our intentions have energy and can shape our reality. Or to put it another way: what you think about, you bring about.

You can try this with an animal who needs a new home or

better situation. Tell the animal intuitively to ask for what she wants in life and start imagining having it. Those two thought processes will set things in motion. If you want to be more elaborate, you can also manifest along with the animal, seeing her in a better situation and feeling how great that would be for her. If you get other people to do this, too, it adds to the effect.

I did this with several people at a stable where I boarded once, when one of the boarders abandoned her perfectly good horse. The stable owner decided to take the horse to auction and sell her for dog meat. We all got together with the horse, explained to her how to manifest for a better future, and went to work ourselves. We imagined the horse with a new person in a great new home. We felt how wonderful it would be to see her get on a trailer and ride off with her new person. All week we kept on thinking and feeling this way whenever we thought of the horse. At the end of the week, a woman who had heard about the horse offered to take her to a fantastic new home.

ASSISTING FERAL ANIMALS

Often, intuitive communication is the only way to approach a feral dog or cat who mistrusts humans. Madeline Runion has found it useful in her rescue work with feral cats. She traps cats, gets them spayed and neutered, and finds caregivers for them. One female cat she trapped turned out to be pregnant. Madeline put her in a room in her home that she uses for fostering cats. The female gave birth to four kittens, but instead of the nice box Madeline had for her, she chose to give birth in the bottom of a cat tree that had hardly any room for her, let alone four kittens. When Madeline went to feed the cat, she would hiss, warning Madeline to stay away. One of the babies died and Madeline wanted to remove it, but the cat wouldn't let her near.

So Madeline decided to try using intuitive communication. She went in the room, got down to eye level with the cat, and told her that she really needed to remove her dead baby before it made her other babies sick. Madeline said that she loved the cat and her babies and that the cat needed to move her babies over to the nice box she had fixed up. Madeline pointed to the box and left the room. When she came back a few minutes later, she found the cat spread out full-length in her new box with her chin resting on her paws. Her babies were still in the cat tree. Madeline got down next to the cat at eye level again. This time the cat didn't hiss. Madeline told the cat she wanted to move the babies for her. Then she picked up each kitten and put it against the cat's belly. The cat didn't hiss or move. She was totally relaxed, as if she knew Madeline meant no harm. Madeline said it was the most wonderful feeling in the world.

FINDING OUT ABOUT A SHELTER ANIMAL'S PAST

One of the most helpful things you can do for rescue animals is to ask them about their past. You can find out about past owners, past abuse and trauma, and even where they were and what they were called. When Kate Wilcox visited one of the rescue staging areas in New Orleans, there were lots of dogs and cats in crates, and no one knew their names. She spent time with each animal, asking, "What did your person call you?" Since the animals responded to the names she got from them, she kept asking for names and trusting what she received. People would ask her how she knew what an animal's name was, and she would say, "Look to their reactions. If the animal responds, then it must be accurate."

Cali

Rebecca Trono used her skills to figure out the case of a dog with unexplainable personality quirks. The dog was named Cali, and the shelter staff hoped Rebecca could communicate with Cali to help her overcome her unwanted behaviors. Cali refused to climb up stairs, but she would walk down them, although uneasily. She would not cross over visible thresholds, and she could not tolerate confined spaces. Other than that she was a sweet, loving dog that everyone was rooting for. Rebecca connected with Cali, asking if she could show Rebecca where she came from, and what kind of treatment she had received. Immediately Rebecca saw a picture of Cali as a puppy, being half-dragged up a staircase by what appeared to be a youngster. The child was attempting to bring Cali upstairs, and the dog would slip from his grasp and tumble down the stairs, only to be picked up and brought upstairs again. Rebecca clearly got a strong impression from Cali that going up the stairs meant "pain" and going down the stairs meant "escape."

Rebecca then saw Cali, a bit older, enclosed in a closet with sliding doors. Each time Cali would try to exit the closet, first putting her head out, the doors would slam on her head and neck. Rebecca could see the track on the floor that the door slid on. Each time Cali crossed it, she was intentionally hurt. Then, Rebecca got a picture of Cali trapped behind what looked to be a large sheet of plywood. In the picture, someone was throwing their weight against the plywood, so that Cali would be crushed between the wall and the plywood. The pictures were horrible. Rebecca sent Cali healing energy. She told Cali to ask for the kind of home she would like, with nice people and no more abuse. They both agreed that a home with no stairs would be perfect. "Good luck with that!" Rebecca thought to herself as she left the session with Cali.

Rebecca told the shelter behaviorist what she'd found out from Cali, and the staff continued to try to retrain the dog to use the stairs, but with little success. Cali stayed at the shelter for several weeks, and Rebecca was so busy she didn't have time to check on her progress. One afternoon, she was chatting with the staff and asked if anything had happened about a placement for Cali. Rebecca was told that Cali had been adopted, and that one of the behaviorists spoke with the prospective new owners. She said to them, "Are you aware that this dog will not climb stairs?"

"Oh, that's not an issue for us at all," the couple said, "We live in a ranch home that is all one level. We don't have any stairs!"

HELPING THE SPIRIT OF A TRAUMATIZED ANIMAL

One technique that I have used a lot with animals who have been abused and traumatized is what I call Spirit Talk. It involves working with the unseen world of the higher-self and spirit guides. If these ideas seem a bit too airy for you, you can skip to the next section, as this technique is not essential to helping such animals. But if you want to try it, here's how.

Ask the animal what happened in the past to make her so angry and/or afraid. Once you discover that, ask her to describe the people or animals involved and tell you how she feels about what they did to her. Ask if she would be willing to go with you in spirit to talk with these people or animals and tell them how she feels. Assure her she will be safe and suggest that by doing this she will be able to go forward with her life and leave the abuse behind. Ask your spirit guides to come along and invite the animal to do the same. Spirit guides are the spirits of relatives, friends, or animals who have died, or any other helpful spirit that is watching over and protecting you.

In your imagination, travel together with the animal to a place in nature you know of that feels sacred to you. Meet with the higher-selves of the people or animals who did the abuse. They can have their spirit guides with them, too. Ask the animal to tell the people or animals how she feels about what happened. Usually there will be quite an outpouring of emotion. Tell the animal to wait for a response. Sometimes there will be a resolution, sometimes not. Ask the animal to say whatever else she wants. Explain that what was done to her was done by people or animals who were stuck in abusive behavior and unable to get out. If they could have acted better, they would have. Ask her to see this and to send energy to those who abused her to promote their healing. Explain that what is needed is for them to shift so that other animals won't have to suffer in the same way. Ask her to see the abusers turn and leave her, going away from her forever. Return with the animal to the present time and space.

HELPING YOUR OWN ANIMALS IN DISTRESS

Your own animals can have trauma and crises, too, and when that happens, you will be better prepared to help them if you can communicate intuitively with them.

Goldie and Isis

Cheryl Paulus decided she needed to try talking intuitively with her own cats, who were not handling her trips away from home very well. Cheryl couldn't understand why they were having a problem. Whenever she went away, her cats would be fed by a friend. They had access to the outdoors and all the things they had when Cheryl was home, except her. Since cats sleep twenty hours a day (by some estimates), she couldn't understand why they were so upset. Her cat Goldie wouldn't even eat while she was away. And her other cat, Isis, acted distant and unfriendly when Cheryl returned home.

Cheryl began using intuitive communication to prepare the cats for her trips, explaining where she was going, why she had to travel, who would be taking care of them, and how long she would be gone. While she was away, she checked in intuitively with each cat every day, telling them what she was doing and when she would be back. As soon as she began these practices, Goldie started eating while she was away, and Isis forgave her quickly upon her return. Cheryl always talks to them now when she has to travel. She's also begun to ask them what they are doing and how they are feeling, and she is getting better and better at picking up their responses.

ASSISTING ANIMALS WITH PHYSICAL PROBLEMS

The stories in this section show how intuitive communication can be used to help an animal who has physical problems. It is encouraging to see that many veterinarians are learning to use these techniques in their practices. A friend and former student, Madeline Yamate, who is now a holistic veterinarian, told me she uses intuitive communication all the time with the animals she treats. She says hello to the animals before she starts to touch and palpate them, and asks for their permission to allow her to help them. When she is going to insert an acupuncture needle at a strong point, she tells the animal out loud that the next point may hurt. She said she has only had an animal react badly to a strong point twice, by turning around, looking, and yelping. In both cases she had forgotten to warn the animal about the point in advance. Madeline asks for the animals' help when she has to draw blood or take a urine sample, explaining what she will be doing and why she has to do it.

Madeline and her dogs

She has found that talking out loud about death with animals who are terminally ill helps both the animal and the person. Often, after such a discussion, a terminal animal will touch the top of his head to Madeline's heart. She feels the animal is saying, "Thank you. I am ready to pass in peace."

Isabelle

Lisa Hartnett practices chiropractic with humans and energy healing and communication with animals. Using intuition, she explains to animals what she needs from them and what she will be doing. Lisa told me about a Bernese mountain dog named Isabelle who had injured herself on a hike. When Lisa arrived, Isabelle was more interested in playing than in receiving healing. Lisa explained to Isabelle in words and pictures why she was there and the time limit she

Lisa with a client

had. She made it clear that she didn't have time to play. She then sat in a chair across the room from Isabelle and told the dog that if she wanted Lisa's help she would have to come to her. Isabelle dramatically changed her demeanor, and after a few minutes she came over and lay down under Lisa's hands and relaxed for her treatment.

Rune

Marilyn Terry found that animals will come to *you* to communicate when they are in crisis. Her now-deceased Scottish deerhound, Rune, was everything a perfect deerhound should be, except like many other dogs, he hated having his feet handled, especially when Marilyn attempted to cut his nails. To warn her off, he would lie on the couch, head high, with his teeth bared. It was only a show of force, but it was intimidating enough for Marilyn to cease and desist. With Rune, anything to do with his feet was strictly off-limits.

That all changed one summer day, when she noticed him starting to lick his feet. Marilyn thought it was just his allergies acting up. Then he started gnawing at his left foot. Nine days later he hobbled into the kitchen dead-lame. He came painfully limping over to stand beside her, holding his left front foot high, imploring her for help. He stood by the table and let her inspect his foot. She was horrified to discover a mass of foxtails embedded between his toes. They looked into each other's eyes, and Marilyn knew that Rune was saying he would not hurt her because he had asked her for help. She pulled out some foxtails, all bloodied, and then pulled out some more, while Rune stood patiently. She looked at his other front foot and found another mass of bloodied foxtails. At times it was so painful he pulled his feet away and tried to hide.

Eventually he lay on the floor and allowed her to examine all his feet, between all his toes, while she found even more foxtails that must have been festering quite a while. Marilyn could

Rune

not believe she had been so obtuse as to not examine his feet earlier when he was chewing on them.

She then flushed out his wounds using a syringe. All the while Rune lay on his side and tolerated what must have been enormous pain. At times Marilyn's face was inches from his and from those big teeth that had always warned her off, but there was not a murmur from him. Marilyn felt certain that under different circumstances, if Rune had not had such faith in her, he would have had to be tranquilized. For several days after, Marilyn examined Rune's feet to make sure she had gotten all the foxtails out. She and Rune had established a higher level of communication and absolute trust.

The saga didn't end there. Marilyn had to soak Rune's feet in Epsom salts and give him homeopathic remedies to remove the last of the foxtails lodged deep inside. From that point on, Rune allowed her to perform regular foot checks and explore between all his toes. Never again was there a problem touching his feet.

Hurricane Dog

Another story about a dog who was a hurricane victim was sent to me by Cindi Clarke. When Hurricane Ivan hit, Cindi and her husband were at the door looking out and noticed a dog outside who seemed to want to come in. Cindi went out to check and found a large, gaunt male wolf-mix. He was panting, exhausted, and covered in cactus spines. Cindi told him that she was not going to hurt him. She brought him some food and water, and he came over and ate and drank a little. Cindi could see cactus spines stuck in his mouth and feet, and huge spiny berries hanging off his body and underbelly.

Cindi asked him if he would let her take the spines out. He just stood there, so she went in and got a pair of leather gloves, some needle-nosed pliers, and a bucket to drop the cactus in. The dog let her remove the large pieces on his body and some of the looser ones from under his belly. She asked if he would sit so that she could take some of the spines out of his paws, and he sat. She talked to him the entire time and kept telling him how handsome he was, and how brave, and that she wasn't going to hurt him. There were a few times she would pull a cactus spine from between his toes and he would flinch slightly, then get up and walk around the corner. After a moment or two he would return and allow her to continue. It was almost as if he was too much of a gentleman to let her hear him cuss because of the pain. She removed as much as she felt she safely could. Since she already had her own four cats and two dogs in the house, she made a place for him in the garage to ride out the storm.

The next day, she took him to the veterinarian, who removed the remainder of the cacti from the dog's mouth and gums. The dog tested positive for heartworm, but needed to gain some weight before they could start treatment. One of her co-workers at the time had just lost a dog, and Cindi approached him about taking this one. Her co-worker and the dog turned out to be a great match. Now "Eli" has a permanent home, and he successfully underwent heartworm treatment.

The Flu

Marie Rubin, a student of intuitive communication, used her ability to communicate to help a veterinarian treat a difficult case. Marie's local equine veterinarian was called in to help an acutely ill two-year-old filly who would not eat or drink, had a very high fever, and was showing signs of neurologic involvement, with stumbling, pressing her head on the wall, and severe depression. The filly was treated with intravenous fluids, antibiotics, and drugs for the pain and fever, which seemed to help some. She was eating a little, but refused to eat off the ground and would only eat from a hay bag suspended in her stall. The veterinarian's greatest concern was that the filly was showing neurologic symptoms, which is a hallmark of equine herpes. The veterinarian drew blood and took nasal smears, which she sent off to the veterinary laboratory. The owner and the veterinarian continued to treat the horse while waiting for the laboratory results.

In the meantime, the other four horses on the farm began to show similar symptoms. Unfortunately, one of the older horses became so ill and weak that he had to be euthanized. The laboratory work finally came back, and it was negative for herpes. There was still no explanation for the illnesses. Other farms in the area began to report horses with similar symptoms.

Out of frustration, the veterinarian asked Marie to speak with the filly, to try to figure out how she was feeling and to give her some encouragement. Marie spoke with the filly and scanned her body to see if she could get some information. Marie felt the filly had a severe sore at the back of her throat. It felt like slivers of glass, making it hard for the filly to swallow. Marie also felt that she had severe pain all around her eyes, and at the top of her head, which increased when she put her head down; hence the reason why the filly would only eat out of a suspended hay bag, not off the ground. The filly had also been head pressing, which would have made the pain in her head feel better by relieving the pain in her sinuses. After speaking with the filly, Marie sent her energy healing to help her to feel better and keep her spirits up. She told the filly that the veterinarian would take good care of her and she would feel better soon.

When Marie called the veterinarian and told her what she had learned, the veterinarian exclaimed, "Influenza! Those are the signs of influenza!" All the horses tested positive for influenza, even though they had been vaccinated for it. With supportive care, they made a slow, complete recovery. And the veterinarian now regularly calls Marie to speak with her patients, and she even gives out Marie's number to her clients.

Rose

Kendra Wilson told me the following story about Rose, a rescue horse at the Pregnant Mare Rescue[3] ranch in Santa Cruz, California, where Kendra volunteers. When Rose arrived, no one could figure out what was wrong with her. She walked very slowly with her head hanging down. If something was in front of her, she would walk into it: bushes, feed buckets, and other horses. The ranch manager got advice from many experts, and everyone had a different opinion: either Rose was in pain, she had neurological problems, or she was retarded.

Then the ranch had a bodyworker come out. He said that Rose was withdrawn from the world. This made sense to Kendra, since Rose was adopted straight off the slaughterhouse feed lot at only three years old, already pregnant, with feet so overgrown they looked like elves' slippers. No wonder she didn't want to be in the world. The ranch also had a chiropractor come out, and he said that Rose's neck had probably been yanked hard by a lasso. He adjusted her and she seemed a bit better. The ranch trainer began working with Rose, following up with what the bodyworker had done, and Rose started getting a little more alert — she began to lift her head and perk her ears up and even canter around from time to time.

Then one day, Rose sent Kendra an intuitive message. Kendra heard her say mentally, "I'm in pain, and I don't want to be in the world anymore." Kendra felt that Rose's pain was all over her body, and much of it was emotional, but she saw it more clearly in Rose's back legs from midleg down to the ground. Then Rose told Kendra that the reason she ran into things, at slow motion, was because it was simply too much effort to go around. What Kendra heard from Rose was, "If you don't want to be somewhere and you're in pain, objects don't really exist." Kendra didn't believe what she was hearing from Rose because much more experienced horse people had been evaluating Rose. Kendra was new to horses and new to intuitive communication. However, soon after she got that message from Rose, the ranch had a natural hoof trimmer come out to work on Rose. The trimmer said that Rose's feet were still overgrown, even though they had been trimmed somewhat; they were out of balance and severely painful, especially the hind legs.

Kendra and Rose

Although she is moving around much better, Rose is still withdrawn. Kendra said that whatever happened to this poor horse must have been pretty bad for her to have displaced her spirit so profoundly. However, Kendra can now see a spark in Rose's eyes from time to time. The most amazing and wonderful part is that she can sometimes see Rose laughing.

Intuitive Troubleshooting

My colleague Gerrie used her ability to converse with animals to help a client with a horse who had digestive problems. One of the woman's mares had had diarrhea for over a month. Gerrie went to the stable and laid out all the foods the mare was eating. Then she went through each food with the horse. Gerrie would touch the food and then ask the horse how she felt about it. Some foods the horse liked, some she didn't like, and some she said she wanted later but not right then. The client then only fed the foods the horse indicated she wanted, and within a day the diarrhea stopped. Gerrie said she does this all the time for animals, even from a distance, and it is a quick and effective method.

EXERCISES FOR TALKING WITH ANIMALS YOU DON'T KNOW

Here are two exercises to help you develop the ability to communicate easily with animals you know nothing about, like rescue animals or the dogs you meet at a dog park.

EXERCISE
Talking with a Shelter Animal

Try talking with the animals in your local shelter. Go to the shelter and find a dog or cat who has been there for a long time whom no one appears to want to adopt.

- Once you've found an animal you want to talk with, take a moment to breathe, relax, and send love from your heart to the animal.
- Have your notebook ready and record any first impressions that are coming to you about this animal.
- Once you have finished the first impressions, introduce yourself, explain what you are doing, and ask for the animal's help. Make sure it feels okay to proceed, and then start talking to the animal by sending thoughts mentally.
- Ask the animal how he or she feels about being in the shelter. Wait for an impression to come from the animal and write it down. Don't go to the next question until you have written something in your notebook. If you aren't getting any impressions, make your best guess about how the animal feels, record that, and go on. Making a guess like this will help get your intuition going.
- Ask where the animal came from, who the previous owners were, and what life was like before coming to the shelter. Record your impressions or your best guess about the answer.

- Ask the animal what he or she would like in a new home. Record your impressions or your best guess about the answer.
- Tell the animal how you feel about what the animal has told you, and give the animal your best advice on how to find a good person and a permanent home, given the animal's history and desires. Listen again and record any impressions.
- When you are finished, thank the animal for talking with you.
- Follow up in a few days or weeks, to check on the animal and see if he or she was adopted.

EXERCISE
Practicing to Get Verification

Here is a general exercise you can use to help you get verification of your accuracy in intuitive communication. To do this exercise, you will need to work with an animal you don't know who has an owner who can verify the answers you get to the questions you ask the animal. Sometimes this person can be a friend or relative, as long as you don't know their animal very well. When you do the exercise, you can communicate in person or from a distance. Before you start, ask if there are any issues or problems the person would like you to discuss with the animal. Jot those down. Then, follow these steps:

- Get the animal's name, age, and sex. If you are not working in person, get a photograph or a description.
- Breathe, relax, and get grounded. Be positive about the outcome.
- Close your eyes, imagine the animal is right there in front of you, and send love from your heart to the animal.
- Record your first impressions.

- Say the animal's name mentally and introduce yourself. Explain to the animal that you are a beginner, and you are learning how to communicate intuitively. Ask if the animal would be willing to talk to you.
- Send a compliment mentally to the animal.
- See if it feels okay to proceed. If not, discuss it a bit further to see if you can get the animal's okay. If you don't get that, go on to another animal.
- If you do get an okay, invite the animal to interact with you in your imagination: pat the animal, give a treat, go for a walk, and so on. Record any further impressions that come to you.
- Ask the animal some verifiable questions and record the responses and impressions you receive. If nothing is coming in, make your best guess as to the answers to the questions. Here are some possible choices for questions:
- What do you like? What do you dislike?
- What other animals do you live with and how do you feel about them?
- Are you worried about anything lately?
- Has anything changed recently?
- What does your house look like?
- Where do you like to sleep?
- Where do you like to go?
- What do people always say about you?
- Now ask the animal the problem or issue questions their person provided. Record any responses and impressions you receive.
- Ask the animal if he or she has a message and record what you get.
- Thank the animal for talking with you and say whatever else you want to communicate to the animal.
- Return to an awake, alert state and check out your answers with the animal's person.

When you start out practicing, and it's time to verify the information you received, make it easy on yourself by asking the animal's person to tell you the correct answers to the verifiable questions first, rather than telling them what you found. Once you see how accurate you've been with these verifiable questions, you can check out the rest of your results.

It will also be very useful to mark your answers as you check your results with the animal's person; this will help convince you that what you're receiving is real. Put a check mark if the answer is correct, a question mark if uncertain, and an X if incorrect. Remember, though, that what the animal tells you may turn out to be accurate, even if the person doesn't think so. The person may simply not know what is true, or may have forgotten. When you get information that is exceptional — something you could not have made up, that must have come from the animal — circle it. Then look back through your notebook every so often. All those check marks and circles will really help convince your rational mind of your accuracy and ability.

CHAPTER 8
Using Intuition to Find a Lost Animal

$\mathcal{F}$inding lost animals using intuitive skills is one of the more difficult things an animal communicator is asked to do. The margin of error seems to be higher with lost animals, and for that reason a lot of professionals choose not to take on lost animal cases. I have consulted about lost animals extensively, and I know that I can be wrong some of the time. Other communicators I know well who I think are competent and accurate also have problems finding lost animals. I don't know anyone who doesn't.

My colleagues and I have speculated that lost animal cases are difficult for a host of reasons: there is intense emotion and drama going on; the situation for the animal can change minute by minute; the animal may be in shock or in a coma; the animal might not know where she is; and the animal may not even know she is dead. These all seem to be valid explanations for why searching intuitively for lost animals isn't as easy as finding out intuitively what your animal loves to do or who her best friends are. I always tell people it is worth hiring a communicator, who can often solve the case, but if money is tight, they should spend it on making and distributing flyers.

Either way, handing out flyers door-to-door is essential: it helps you alert people in your area, so they can be your eyes and ears in your search for your animal. Any other publicity is good as well. I encourage people to use a search dog, too, if there is one available in their area. Check the Resources section (page 187) for more ideas on finding lost animals. There is one resource, however, that you won't find there, and that is your own intuition.

You can use your intuition to talk with your animal, and he or she will hear you, even from a distance. You can work with positive visualization to increase the likelihood of the safe return of your animal. I hope you never have to use such skills, but if you do, this chapter can help.

BE POSITIVE

The first thing to do when your animal becomes lost is to remain positive. Your thoughts are energy, and energy can impact the course of reality. In order to set up the optimal conditions for searching for your lost animal, it is important that everyone involved stay focused on a positive outcome. This can be hard to do, since our tendency when an animal is lost is to assume the worst. We play one hideous scenario after another in our minds: she got run over, someone stole her, a coyote ate her. You could probably come up with negative scenarios all day long without repeating yourself once. All that powerful negative emotion has energy — the wrong kind of energy.

EXERCISE
Be Positive

When you find yourself thinking the worst, stop and say, "Cancel that thought." Then imagine positive scenarios instead: your animal is found by a kind person who calls you, your animal shows up at your door, and so on. Close your eyes and see your animal back home safe and sound. Make sure to feel hope and optimism, as it is feeling even more than visualization that helps shift reality. Feel how it would be to have your animal home again and okay. Do that as often as you can.

Think of a positive phrase that you can say to yourself about your lost animal. It could be something like, "She makes it home safe and sound." Use whatever words make you feel calmer. The goal is to get your energy working for the right outcome. Say your phrase whenever you need to redirect your outlook.

Have your friends imagine the return of your animal, too. Ask them to pray for this and feel it happening. The more people you can get to do this, the better. Also ask the universe, your spiritual guides, your animal's spiritual guides, or whatever power you believe in, to bring your animal back to you.

TALK TO YOUR ANIMAL

The basic principle of intuitive communication is that you can communicate intuitively in person or from a distance. No matter how far away you are from your animal, you can send your thoughts and your animal will receive them. You can send your animal mental instructions for how to find her way home, what to do to be safe, who to approach for help, how to avoid cars, and anything else she needs to know.

Tucker

Pam and Paul Hendricks called me in a panic about their two huskies, a male and female, who had gotten out of the yard and become lost. It turned out that the dogs had gone up into the mountains behind their house and followed some people on horseback. The horseback riders realized the dogs were lost and headed back to where they had parked their trailer. The female dog, Tashi, jumped right into the trailer with the horses. But the male, Tucker, wouldn't come near the people. Then he saw a deer and ran off into the woods. The horseback riders read Tashi's collar and called Pam and Paul to return her. But Tucker remained lost, and that's when Pam called me to ask for help.

I tuned in to Tucker and felt that he was alive, up on the mountain, confused, hungry, and not sure how to get home. I told Pam and Paul to go back to where the horse trailer had been, as I felt that Tucker was coming back there every so often. Paul went back to the area and found fresh scat there that he thought was Tucker's, but he couldn't find Tucker.

Tucker

Later that day, they called me back, and I tuned in to Tucker again. This time, I saw Tucker going over the mountain and down the other side to a creek on the far side. Paul went looking again and found Tucker's tracks in the creek, but no Tucker. At that point it was almost dark. I told Pam and Paul to send Tucker a mental map of the best way to get home, which would have been for him to follow the creek down to the river, then follow the river back to the road where they lived. But this was not a route Tucker had ever been on. They agreed to send him images of taking that route home.

At four o'clock the next morning, Pam was watching outside when she spotted Tucker trotting along the road toward home from the direction of the river. He had heard her instructions and found his way home. He was covered in fly bites and full of porcupine quills, but otherwise okay.

EXERCISE
Bring Them to Safety

As Pam and Paul did with Tucker, you can give your animal instructions on how to get home. Close your eyes and imagine
your animal. Explain out loud to your animal whatever you can
tell her that will help her to safely return to you. Tell her the best
route to take to get home and how to travel it safely. Or, if it
would be better, encourage her to find a good-hearted person
to rescue her. Do this at least once a day during your search.

CLEAR THE WAY HOME

Sometimes animals leave home simply because they have the opportunity: someone left the door open, they found a way out of
the yard, and so on. But sometimes there is something going on in
the home that scared the animal, such as fireworks, another animal attacking them, or workmen or other strangers in the home.
There might even have been a disagreement between the person
and the animal prior to the disappearance, or some change in the
home that the animal did not like.

If you think there was something your animal was afraid of or
upset about that could have had anything to do with her disappearance, it is best to clear that out emotionally. Luckily you can
use intuitive communication to do this, and here's how.

EXERCISE
Clear the Way Home

Find a quiet place, sit with your eyes closed, imagine or feel
your animal as if she is right there with you, and start talking.
Say you are sorry for whatever happened, and make any

promises you know that you can keep about how the situation will change or improve. Follow through and make whatever changes you can immediately while you are still searching for your animal.

SEND ENERGY

There are two visualizations involving energy that I teach people to do when they are searching for a lost animal. The first is to imagine sending a feeling of love and protection to surround and guard your animal. The other is to imagine a magnetic beam of energy linking your heart and your animal's heart, and then to feel that beam pulling you both back together. These energy visualizations can have a positive effect on the outcome of your search and are helpful to both you and your lost animal.

EXERCISE
Energy Visualizations

Close your eyes and imagine your animal. Feel the love you have for that animal and send it over the air to your animal wherever she may be. Imagine her surrounded by that feeling. Now send a feeling of protection to your animal. You might want to imagine it as a color that surrounds and guards her.

In the second visualization, imagine a magnetic beam of energy linking your heart and your animal's heart. Feel that beam pulling you both back together. Believe in the power of that energy beam to do that for you.

FOLLOW YOUR INTUITION

You will get a lot of information from people about what to do and where to search for your animal. You may get a lot of sightings. If you call more than one communicator, you may even have multiple possible scenarios. If this occurs, it would be a good time to tune in to your intuition and follow your own inner guidance.

EXERCISE
Follow Your Intuition

Tune in to your intuition and ask what you need to do to find your animal. Record whatever comes in. Stand outside with your eyes closed and feel which way feels like the right way to go to search for your animal. Then ask how far you need to go. Pay attention to everything that comes in from your intuition, and follow up on it as best you can.

SEARCH WHILE YOU SLEEP

When you sleep, you are closest to your intuition, and you can use your time asleep as a way to search for your animal. People in the midst of a search usually think of sleeping as useless downtime, but instead, see it as useful search time.

EXERCISE
Search While You Sleep

Before you go to sleep, say this intention: "In my sleep I will find out where my animal is and what I need to do to get her back." Have a paper and pen near the bed. When you wake up, record whatever you can remember of your dreams. If you can't recall anything, ask yourself, "What was I just thinking?" Then write whatever comes to you. If you do it consistently over time, this will train you to recall your dreams. Follow up on any leads that come to you in your dreams.

WHEN TO GIVE UP

I tell people not to give up too early. I have had animals turn up weeks and even months after they have disappeared. On the other hand, you can make yourself ill with stress from searching too hard. Do everything you can initially — check the Resources section (page 187) for more recommendations — then visit the shelters and refresh your ads and flyers on a regular but reasonable basis. Once you have done all you can, turn it over to the universe and hope for the best. Follow your intuition about whether to keep searching and how to do that.

FINDING SWERVE

Lori Pichurski struggled with whether to give up when she lost her young herding dog, Swerve, who ran away from a pet sitter's house by jumping the fence. Swerve is a Mudi, a primitive, less-domesticated breed that is shy with people and very clever. Lori did everything to find Swerve. She put up posters, talked to neighbors, walked the neighborhood, talked to the local businesses, the police, the fire department, and the railway patrol, and got the local TV station to do a story. She even got a tracking dog to look for him. The tracking dog scented Swerve going west from the dog sitter's house toward the river, and then lost the scent. Lori had a number of sightings for the first three weeks, then nothing. That's when she called me for help.

I worked on the case and also referred her to one of my colleagues, Karen Berke. Karen and I both felt that Swerve was alive, and we gave Lori a lot of details about where to search. But she still couldn't find him. Lori knew she had good intuition — she could easily read other people's animals — but she had a block when it came to Swerve. One thing she was sure of, though, was that he was alive. She would call on us every once in a while to get more information, and then she would meditate on what we had said. She said that little details would stand out. For instance, I told her that Swerve was west of the river and Karen said that he was near coyotes but not living with them. I told her I saw some big trucks parked in a lot near to where Swerve was, and Karen said that wherever he was there was wild grass and manicured lawn, side by side. Lori's mom helped her search for Swerve, and they would go out and try to find the location based on the details Karen and I gave them.

Lori did a lot of praying about Swerve, calling on the angels that look after animals and lost souls to help. She prayed every day for his safety and sent a feeling of protective energy to him to help guard him from the coyotes.

Six months after Swerve escaped, Lori got a call from an elderly couple who said they had been feeding a dog down by the west side of the river whom they thought was Swerve. They called him a "ghost dog" because he would just disappear the minute they spotted him. Lori didn't know if the dog they sighted was Swerve, but she went prepared. She took clothes she'd recently worn that had her scent, and toys that had been Swerve's. When she got to the couples' house she called Swerve, but there was no response. She left the clothes and toys down near the river. When she came back the next day, all the items had been dragged away. Then she knew that it was Swerve.

Lori was prepared to work gradually at gaining his trust, and she hoped that Swerve would remember her or her voice. When she got to the couples' house the next day, she had her first sighting of Swerve in six months. She went down on one knee and called to him, tossing a tennis ball, one of his favorite toys, in the air. Swerve circled her and came back toward her. She called again and then he jumped into her arms, kissing her. She said everything about him was frozen and frosted. He was like an icicle. She asked Swerve if he wanted to go for a ride, and her heart stopped when he jumped up and ran away from her.

Then she saw he was just headed toward her truck. She opened the truck door and he jumped into the passengers' seat, ready to go. At home that night and at the training center the next day, he played and interacted with the other dogs and people as if he had only been gone for a day.

Swerve was in an area west of the river, which is what I saw. The area had wild grass that also bordered on a golf course, which is the information Karen received. The couple who was feeding him had a number of big trucks parked next to their house, which is what I saw. And as Karen had seen, Swerve was in an area where he had to cohabitate with two different coyote packs who were chasing him. The energy protection Lori sent had done a good job.

Everyone who had been helping Lori look for Swerve gave up except for her mother. Lori's friends and associates told her

that she was obsessed with Swerve and advised her to abandon her search and get back to training her other dogs. But Lori knew in her heart that Swerve was still alive. Swerve is a clever, wonderful dog, who by some miracle survived that ordeal. He now sticks like glue to Lori wherever they go.

Swerve

CHAPTER 9
Coping with Death

*T*he hardest part of having animals is losing them; it is the price we pay for the incredible experience of sharing their lives. I have lost a number of animals so far in my life, and I realize that I have become smarter about death. I understand it better and accept it more. Each animal's death I've gone through has taught me something different, like when to let go, how to make the decision, how to feel the spirit leave the body, how to survive grief, and how to connect once the body is gone. I think animal lovers are some of the best-educated people about death on the planet. One thing for certain I have learned is that intuitive communication makes the whole process of death easier from start to finish — as easy as it can get.

People often call me wanting advice about whether to assist their animal in dying. I tell them to base their decision on the animal's quality of life. If it is much reduced, it might be time to help the animal die. Try to assess how much your animal is suffering. For example, if your animal is in pain that can't be relieved, has stopped eating and is starving to death, or can't get up anymore, it might be more merciful to let him or her go. I am not a believer in natural death at any price. Then again, some animals do have a very peaceful death process and don't need help to die.

This is where intuitive communication comes in handy. You can ask your animal what she wants and she will tell you. I recall well my conversation with my black Lab Daisy on the morning when she could no longer get up. I asked if she wanted to go now, and she very definitely said she did. I was certain that it was the right time to let her go, even though I probably could have kept her alive longer. She did not want to stay alive and be unable to get up, that just wasn't something she wanted to do. Other animals may be okay with that. You will have to tune in to your emotions and your intuition and go with what feels right for you and your animal. It will be up to you two to make the decision about when life ends.

WHEN IS IT TIME TO GO?

Being able to hear your animal helps enormously, as you will see in the following two stories from Irene Bras, who works as a professional animal communicator. Several years ago Irene rescued two cats from Italy. One of the cats, Lohengrin, was very ill, but Irene was certain he would make it in spite of the fact that everyone around her encouraged her to euthanize him. When she got him, she had just taken some classes from me and was still insecure about her own intuitive capacities, until one day, six months after she had rescued him. That afternoon she heard him say very clearly, "I want to transition now." He also communicated to her that he had come to be with her to die in peace after having experienced what it felt like to be loved. Irene immediately made an appointment with a veterinarian to help Lohengrin die. She said she is still grateful for the support she received from him on her intuitive path.

Another cat of Irene's, Tjalinka, became ill and started to lose weight rapidly. It turned out that her kidneys were failing. Irene began intensive care for her, which included hand-feeding her three times a day. A special bond grew between them, and Irene admired Tjalinka for her positive attitude. One day she began to worry about Tjalinka. Images of what might come to pass ran through her mind. When Tjalinka noticed this, she told Irene that this was not the way to go. She said she needed freedom in order to be able to decide for herself when it was her time to leave.

She asked Irene to live in the moment, continue cherishing what they had, and stop worrying about what they might lose. Irene realized this was a trend in life: to worry about what you might lose, rather than appreciating what you have.

Irene and her dog

Once Irene realized this, Tjalinka was free to make her own decisions about when it was time to go. Tjalinka's death went easily. Without difficulty she completed her journey all by herself, and before she died, she told Irene that she wanted to be cremated. Irene hadn't had time to discuss with her whether she wanted to be buried or cremated, but then Tjalinka gave her the answer she needed.

EXERCISE
Finding Out What Your Animal Wants

Before your animal dies, ask what she wants for her death. Does she want a party with all your friends there and everyone dancing? Does she want to be buried, and if so, where? Does she want to be cremated? Record whatever impressions you get about her wishes.

You can also get your animal's input on the decision about whether or not to euthanize. Ask your animal to tell you whether she wants help with dying. Record your impressions immediately and assume they are coming from your animal. If your animal does want help with the dying process, ask if she can give you a sign when the time comes, so you will know she is ready to have help. Ask her to make it something obvious. Record whatever impressions come to you about what this sign will be.

SAYING GOOD-BYE

It helps to prepare for death. One of the first things to do is to make sure you've said everything to your animal that you want her to know. Tell her how much you have loved her and all the things she did for you in your life.

EXERCISE
Let Them Know You Love Them

Using intuitive communication, tell your animal everything you love about her, everything you have learned from her, and the reasons you are happy she has been in your life. Listen to what she has to say. Pay attention to any impressions coming your way and record them. Assume they are from your animal. This exercise is especially useful once you know your animal is dying. If your animal dies a sudden death, you can always have this talk with your animal in spirit. It is never too late to tell your animals that you love them, no matter how much time has passed.

WHEN THEY LEAVE

Some people tell me that they find it very difficult to be with their animals during the dying process. I understand, but I think they are missing out on something important. I have found it to be a profound and healing experience to sit with an animal during death and to stay with the body afterwards. I will stay for as long as it takes to get a sense of the animal's spirit leaving or being outside of the body. For some animals, that happens right away; others take longer. When you can feel your animal's spirit, you realize that your animal is never completely gone from you. That is a lesson our animals want us to learn.

Leo

Lynne Kasuba and Corky Ferris took their cues from their cat Leo when he came to the end of his life. Lynne describes Leo as a willful cat who would tap on your leg until he got what he wanted. He was a funny character with an international fan club. Lynne said she and her husband were completely broken up the day the veterinarian told them Leo was in kidney failure. Still, Leo acted as if nothing were wrong. They noticed him going into the garden alone more, going places he had not been before, and just sitting for hours. They felt that he was saying good-bye to the joy of his world: the beauty, the smells, and the people.

Leo stayed strong and ate well for four months after his diagnosis. They gave him fluids every day, and he actually gained weight. But on the last day, they knew it was different. He didn't want the fluids; he didn't even want hand-feeding from Corky. Lynne followed Leo's every move that day. When she held him, his golden eyes never wavered from hers. Then he turned over like a kitten, and tucked his head into the crook of her arm. Leo loved to be loved. Lynne learned that being near to a dying animal is much better than being far away.

The final night of his life, Lynne and Corky said good night and put Leo on his couch. Leo couldn't walk or jump at that point. They told him they loved him, that it was okay to leave if he needed to, and that they would see him again. The next morning they found his body in front of the fireplace, stretched out.

They watched over him all day. Orange butterflies appeared out of nowhere and came to all the screens and windows. They were sure it was a sign from Leo's spirit. They cried all day and reminisced about him. At the end of the day, they had his funeral. They placed him in a beautiful silk pillowcase Lynne had made, and they buried him where Corky could watch over him while he worked. They said a prayer as the butterflies swarmed all around in an unusual display

Lynne and Leo

that had not happened before and has not happened since. Lynne said that she and Corky know Leo is still with them in spirit. They have even glimpsed him out of the corner of their eyes, and felt his presence on the bed at night.

DEALING WITH GRIEF

The only way to get out of grief is to go through it; otherwise it stays with you, locked inside your body. Realize that you will be devastated when your animal dies and that it will take time to work through it, but that you can and will survive it. It helps to use calming herbs like chamomile tea, and flower essences like rescue remedy. The homeopathic remedy Ignacia amara can also be helpful, as well as lavender essential oil used as aromatherapy. You can find these aids at your local health food store.

Take special care of your body and your emotions when you are grieving. Do aerobic exercise, get massages, and take hot tubs and saunas to help move the grief through your system. Get lots of sleep. Rent some funny movies to make yourself laugh again, but let yourself cry as much as you need to. Realize that some people will not understand what you are going through. Avoid talking to people who aren't supportive. If you have no one to confide in, check with local animal organizations to find a therapy group for people who have lost their animals.

You may find that your surviving animals will grieve as much as you do for the animal who has died. Talk to them about what has happened and console them as best you can. Some of the same things that help you will also help them, like massage and exercise. You can work with a holistic veterinarian to find emotional remedies including herbs, essences, and homeopathics.

CONNECTING WITH SPIRIT

What has helped me the most to deal with my animals' deaths, of all the things I have tried, is the realization that my animals were only gone in body: their spirits are still right here with me, forever. Now I talk with the spirits of animals who have died. I know they are out there hearing me and can respond. I ask for signs from them to help me know they are there. The signs are my proof that their spirits are still with me. This helps me get on with life and leave the grief behind.

Cherokee

Barb Fenwick sent me this story about connecting with the spirit of her horse. She said it was quite possibly the saddest day of her life when she had to put down Cherokee, her sixteen-year-old Appaloosa. He had been poorly cared for in his life and had suffered physical damage that she was unable to help him with. When she decided to put him down, it was because he was in intense pain and his breathing was so labored that she felt it was cruel to keep him alive any longer.

Cherokee didn't seem to question her motives as she dished him out a huge breakfast of oats and sweet alfalfa hay, which were not items on his regular diet. In the distant pasture, a tractor was digging a hole big enough to fit a horse. She led Cherokee and his best friend, a spotted Tennessee walking horse, Spirit, out to pasture and stopped on the crest of a small hill that was well-secluded and chosen with care. The local veterinarian was there, and her good friend and neighbor who had dug the hole, and her husband — all in their own ways prepared to deal with and accept what they were there to do. She took her last walk with Cherokee, down into the giant hole, and said good-bye to a horse that was really too young to die, but who had suffered long enough. His lungs, which had been damaged from heaves (a bronchial disease) made each breath labored and painful. She spoke to him softly through tears as they said farewell. He stood quietly as the veterinarian injected the liquid that would swiftly and humanely end his life. Spirit watched from above; his good-bye to Cherokee was silent to their ears. It was an equally sad day for her neighbor, who had chosen that day and place to also put to rest his faithful, aged dog, Sam. Cherokee and the dog were laid to rest together on "Cherokee Hill."

Summer passed into winter and the pasture where Cherokee was buried became Barb's cross-country ski trails. One day she decided to take a break and strap on her skis for a trip around the property. She had gone only a short distance and was near Cherokee Hill when she heard the urgent twittering of a chickadee. It buzzed over her head and landed on a branch almost within arm's reach. It sat there chattering as she paused, then flew up ahead on the trail, still in the shadow of Cherokee Hill. There it seemed to wait for her and again swooped over her head and landed on a branch so close that Barb could have touched it. The woods and hills were otherwise silent; the only life apparent was this persistent bird that sat there chirping loudly as if to convey an urgent message. Finally it flew off. Then a quarter of a mile farther, it was with her again, this time almost landing on her shoulder and sweeping past to land on a fence post nearby, perching again to sing briefly, then disappearing across the field. It was truly amazing, but she didn't give it much more thought as she continued to break trail with her skis.

The next day she went snowshoeing on the same trail with a friend. When they came to the same place on the trail where the chickadee had last appeared, Barb spotted something in the snow directly in their path. As they approached, she recognized it as a bird's nest. She couldn't figure out what a bird's nest was doing in the middle of the field in winter. There were no trees around. Barb's friend said, "Pick it up. Maybe it's good luck or something." Barb absentmindedly put it in her backpack, and they continued on. She had forgotten all about it until the next day when she emptied her pack. She pulled out the nest and casually examined it. There, artfully interwoven in the fine fibers of the nest were horsehairs — not just any horsehairs, but *Cherokee's* mane and tail hair. Of all Barb's horses, only he had the golden tinge to his hair, distinct as the spots on his rump. Her other horses all had black or white tail and mane hair. It suddenly dawned on her that the visits from the chickadee had very special meaning.

Cherokee

Finding a nest with Cherokee's hair woven into it in the middle of a field in winter right in her path was not a coincidence; it was a message. Barb felt it was Cherokee, come to tell her that he was just fine. She said she knew then that he wasn't really gone, he had just taken wings.

Dylan

No one taught me the lesson that the spirit lives on better than my horse Dylan. Even though he was twenty-three when he died, I was devastated. I think it was because I had tried to fix Dylan's physical problems the whole time I had him, and I was never able to get him completely healed. My dream was to ride the trails with him, and we did only a bit of that in his lifetime. I hated to give up on that dream, as we were so close to achieving it. I had gotten over my fear of riding him and had trained him to be calm on the trail. The problem was his body. He was insulin-resistant and had developed laminitis.[1] I found out after his death that he had multiple internal fatty tumors that caused an obstruction and prevented him from being able to process food.

Marta and Dylan

When it became clear that he could not survive, I told the veterinarians to euthanize him. I had said good-bye many times by then, but I was still overcome by grief.

A few days after he died I started hearing a song in my head. I didn't know the name of it, but I knew a friend who did, so I called her and asked. She said the song was called "Touched by a Rose from the Grave." Right after I found out the name of the song, roses started to bloom all over my property. Then people started giving me roses and sending me cards with roses. I told Dylan, "Okay, I get it. You are still here." For months, whenever I turned on the radio at the barn, that song would be playing. Several times when I drove past the turnoff to the veterinary clinic where he spent his last days, the song would come on the radio. When my trimmer came to do my other horses, we turned on the radio and the song came on again.

Apparently that wasn't enough proof. Dylan wanted me to have more. One day when I was down in the barn in the stall that was his, crying yet again, I looked up to see hundreds of dragonflies swarming all around. I had never seen that before at my place. It happened one more time when my trimmer was there, the same day the song came on the radio. I had a talk with Dylan and told him that it was fantastic that he was giving me so many signs. I told him that I finally really got it: I could be sad but not too sad because he was still, and always would be, right there with me in spirit.

Then he gave me the final sign, his gift to me really. My trimmer Tiffany, and another friend, Sarah, called me up and said, "We are bringing you a horse. You can't say no. He will die where he is. Come see him and we will bring him up to you this week." I went to look. He was a very sick-looking Arab who was underweight, and he had been severely bitten and kicked by the mare he was pastured with. He had chronic diarrhea and a horrible swayback, and he looked as old as the hills. Tiffany was right: if we didn't save him, he probably would not last. So I agreed.

Marta and Rio

After they brought him to me, they told me he had been an endurance horse, but I didn't think much about that, as I assumed he couldn't ever be ridden again. I was wrong. As soon as I switched his diet, his diarrhea stopped and he started gaining weight. With Tiffany's trims, his feet got better. On my property he could get a lot of exercise and walk up and down hills, so his back improved and he started to regain his muscles. Most of all he had hope again, and before my eyes he grew young. Rio and I have now gone horse camping together, another dream of my life, and ridden a few miles. We have a way to go, but I am living the dream with Rio that I wanted to live with Dylan, and I know without a doubt that Dylan sent Rio to me. It was his gift to me for my love of him.

EXERCISE
After They Have Gone

After your animal is gone, tell your animal how much you miss him and how hard it is for you. Apologize if something did not go as well as you wanted during his life or during the death process. Ask your animal for signs that he is still around and watching over you.

Now listen to what he has to say. Pay attention to any impressions coming your way and record them. Assume they are coming from your animal. And pay attention to any signs that may be coming from your animal to prove to you that he is still there watching over you.

COMING BACK?

I didn't start out in this field believing that animals could reincarnate and come back to you in a different body, but after years of talking with animals and hearing people's experiences, I now believe this to be the case. I know many people find this hard to accept, or it is contrary to their beliefs. I am not trying to convince anyone, but merely presenting what I now believe to be true about life after death.

I believe that our animals love being with us, and they come back to be with us over and over in this lifetime and in future lifetimes. I also believe that they find their way to us; we don't have to do much except to pay attention and react appropriately when we sense that there is some unusual connection or situation with an animal we encounter. When my animals die, I tell them that I would love to have them back and ask them to please find me and make it obvious to me if and when they return. It is their decision. Then I let go and wait to see what happens.

I am still waiting for Dougal, the chocolate wolfhound I described in chapter 6, to come back. I got a strong sense from him that he wanted to be a very tiny dog in his next life. It has been a few years since he died and nothing has happened yet. But I am being careful not to rush it. Dougal will come back if and when he is ready, and he will find me and make it obvious, of that I am sure. Maybe I will find a little dog abandoned in the road, or a friend will call and say they have a little dog they can't keep. Somehow I am sure Dougal will be with me again.

In my book *Beyond Words*, I include a chapter of stories people sent or told to me about how their animal had returned, along with the proof they had to back up the claim. Here is one of my favorite stories from that chapter.

Cisco

Jeanne Owen met Cisco when she was out shopping for a new horse. The ad sounded perfect: gentle, gaited, paint gelding. But when she went to see him, he was backed into a corner of an arena and scared to death. She got feelings of anger, defensiveness, and potential violence from him. Not exactly her dream horse. She looked at him and thought, "This can't be the horse I am supposed to have. He doesn't match my mental picture." When the owner came over, Jeanne told him she wasn't interested after all and turned to leave. Then she heard a voice say, "But you don't understand. I'm Danny." Danny was the name of a much-loved Welsh pony Jeanne owned as a child. She wheeled back around and told the owner that on second thought she would take another look.

The owner rode Cisco around the arena, and then agreed to let Jeanne ride the horse out on the trail. She had a remarkable ride and felt totally safe on this horse that a short while before she had decided was not right for her. They rode for over an hour and Cisco was absolutely calm. When she got back to the ranch, the owner greeted her, amazed that she had not had any problems with the horse bucking or rearing. She decided right then and there to buy Cisco and told the man she'd take him.

As Jeanne walked Cisco to the horse trailer, the owner told her to wait while he got a whip to load the horse into the trailer. When the man left, Jeanne looked at Cisco and told him that if he wanted to go with her, he'd better get into the trailer right away. He walked right in. The owner returned with a whip and stud chain and asked in an astonished voice, "How did you get him to load?"

"I just asked him nicely," Jeanne replied.

She and Cisco got along well, but Jeanne was still mystified by the voice she had heard claiming to be Danny. One day about two weeks later she was sitting at a picnic table and Cisco

Jeanne and Cisco

was grazing untied nearby. She turned to him and said, "So, you really are Danny, huh?" Cisco brought up his head, stopped grazing, and walked over to the picnic table. He stood right at the end of the table and nudged her away with his nose. He put both front feet onto the table as if he were going to get up on it. Then he lowered his nose to the table and waited for Jeanne

to react. She laughed and cried simultaneously as she recognized the trick. She and her brother had taught their pony Danny to put his front feet up onto a railing. With his feet up on the railing, they then taught Danny to lower his head between his feet to take a bow. Here was this horse telling Jeanne, "Okay. Here's the proof. Remember this?"

Jeanne said she is sure Danny and she have found each other again, only this time his name is Cisco.

EXERCISE
Are You Coming Back?

Tell your animal that you would love to have her come back to you in another body. Tell her what you would like her to be if she could. Also tell the universe what you want. Now ask your animal to make sure she comes and finds you and that she makes it very clear to you that she is back. Let the request go; release it to the universe.

Now listen to what your animal has to say. Pay attention to any impressions coming your way and record them. Are you getting any intuitive sense of whether she wants to come back, when that might be, what she wants to come back as (her ideas might be different than yours!), and what sign she will give you when she returns? Write down any impressions you get and file them away mentally. If later on down the road something unusual happens with an animal coming into your life, pay attention. It may be one of your animals coming back to be with you.

CHAPTER 10
Intuitive Voice in the Wilderness

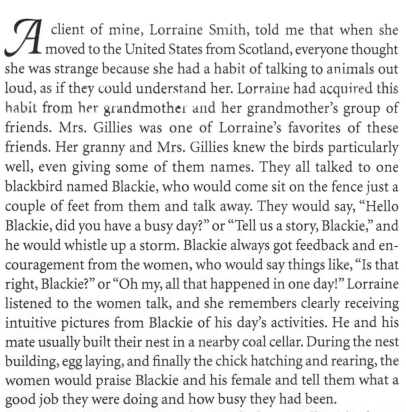

A client of mine, Lorraine Smith, told me that when she moved to the United States from Scotland, everyone thought she was strange because she had a habit of talking to animals out loud, as if they could understand her. Lorraine had acquired this habit from her grandmother and her grandmother's group of friends. Mrs. Gillies was one of Lorraine's favorites of these friends. Her granny and Mrs. Gillies knew the birds particularly well, even giving some of them names. They all talked to one blackbird named Blackie, who would come sit on the fence just a couple of feet from them and talk away. They would say, "Hello Blackie, did you have a busy day?" or "Tell us a story, Blackie," and he would whistle up a storm. Blackie always got feedback and encouragement from the women, who would say things like, "Is that right, Blackie?" or "Oh my, all that happened in one day!" Lorraine listened to the women talk, and she remembers clearly receiving intuitive pictures from Blackie of his day's activities. He and his mate usually built their nest in a nearby coal cellar. During the nest building, egg laying, and finally the chick hatching and rearing, the women would praise Blackie and his female and tell them what a good job they were doing and how busy they had been.

Lorraine's grandmother also taught her to talk with plants.

"You have to talk to the plants if you want them to grow," she would say. She told Lorraine to water plants slowly, stay quiet, and listen, and she would be able to hear them drink. The women could also tell the weather, either by what the animals were doing, what the sky was doing, or what their bodies were doing. Lorraine said these were strong women, and that she misses them as teachers. They made everything so simple and effortless for her.

These things seem strange to people who have grown up in the last fifty years or so, but prior generations were much more connected to the old ways, which included a natural intuitive exchange between humans and the other beings in our environment. People in ancient indigenous cultures related to animals and nature as equals or relatives. If you want to shift your worldview from modern to ancient, you can begin by relating to each lifeform you encounter as if it were as intelligent as you and capable of experiencing the same range and depth of emotions that you do. Then use your intuition to navigate in this alternative world where everything is alive, aware, equal, and related.

Talking intuitively to wildlife and nature is a lot like the talking you have done with your own animals, your friends' animals, and the animals you may be helping at a shelter or helping to rescue. The difference is that it will be harder to get verification of the information you receive. Again, your only option is to accept the impressions that come to you and trust that they are coming from whoever you were talking with intuitively.

TALKING WITH WILDLIFE

Sometimes you will be able to get verification of your impressions by observing the behavior of the wild animal you are communicating with. Colleague Petra Gout told me a story of saving a frog that got wedged between the planks on her front porch. Unable to dislodge the frog, she had to dismantle the planks in order to save him. She explained what was happening to him, and he immediately ceased struggling. Petra said he obviously understood her, and that he was amazingly clever and polite. He waited calmly for her to get the planks apart, and at one point even appeared to bow to her. Once she had freed him from the porch, she put him in a bucket with some water and took him to a nearby shaded pond where he would be safe. As she held him in her hand one last time, looking into his eyes, he reached up and touched his nose to hers.

Kendra Wilson had a similar experience with a grasshopper. She found herself without an animal a few years back. She was living in a cottage surrounded by wildlife at the time, so to fill the gap she made friends with lizards, bugs, and birds, all of whom seemed quite comfortable sitting near her on the deck. She had conversations with them out loud and treated them as her companions. One grasshopper in particular began following her around inside the house. When she woke up in the morning, he would be there, directly above her head on the windowsill. When she made coffee, he would follow her and sit on the counter. She began feeding him some of her morning smoothie, placing a teaspoonful on the counter for him to lick up. When she went into the bathroom, he would follow and perch himself on a shelf above the sink. The grasshopper had been visiting for about two weeks when he decided to begin walking around on the floor. Kendra worried that someone would step on him. Unfortunately, her fiancé accidently did, and he still feels awful about it to this day. Kendra said that even though it was a sad ending, what she remembers most is that it was her first experience of certainty in communicating intuitively with animals.

One avenue for getting verification when talking with insects or wildlife is to ask questions about the biology of the animal and then look up the answers in a field guide. We did something similar when I took a group of people to communicate with gray whales in Mexico. We asked the whales about their migration and how it went. The whales told us it was a hard migration and that several of the mothers had their babies en route rather than in the birthing lagoons. We checked with the naturalist who was with us on the trip, and he confirmed that this can happen at times, and that not all the young whales are born in the lagoons.

A lot of people have sent in stories to me about using intu-itive communication to control insects and rodents around the house and garden. Reysha Silverhair used it with good results in dealing with an excess of spiders in his home. One day, he tuned in to one of the spiders who was sitting on the wall next to his bed. "Little Cousin," he said to her, "let me make a deal with you and all your tribe living on this property. If you will carefully stay out of my space and out of my sight, you may do all your spider-things with no interference from me. If any one or more of you ignores this or violates the agreement, I will transport the offender to an unfriendly location or, if circumstances warrant, kill. Let's make a mutual agreement; you stay out of my space and I will not exter-minate or otherwise harass you. Okay?" Reysha said there was about a three-minute pause for reflection, and then he got an "okay" message from the spider. Since that talk perhaps twice he has seen a spider wander in to look the house over. Each time, he addressed the stray with a quick rundown of the local ground rules and suggested that she join in or move on — quickly. An hour or two seemed all that was required before the spider then disappeared.

Gerrie Huijts communicates with the ants to get them to move out of her kitchen and cellar, although she said it takes a while and can require several conversations. She once warned a nest of wasps in the attic that if they didn't move, they would be killed, and the wasps were gone within an hour. Gerrie's latest intuitive commu-nication project involves training flies to sit on her finger so she can escort them out of the house. She said making deals is a tech-nique that has worked well with moles. She had a problem with moles, but since she also loves them, she didn't want to tell them to go away. Instead, she talked with them and worked out an agreement that when traveling, they would only go along the walls of her house, not right across the yard. In return, Gerrie would allow them to dig holes and eat whatever they wanted on the perimeter of the yard. So far the moles are keeping up their end of the bargain. There was one small molehill that popped up in the middle of the yard again, and when she asked about it, the mole who was responsible apologized, saying he was new in the area, in a hurry, and not aware of the agreement. Gerrie reports that moles are very polite animals.

You can encourage the kind of wildlife you want to have in your yard, such as birds, butterflies, dragonflies, and squirrels, by setting up feeding and watering stations and plantings to attract them. When you talk to the wildlife in your backyard, use the techniques you have already learned: introduce yourself, start talking, and record whatever impressions come to you.

I have found wildlife to be a bit more philosophical in conversation than domesticated animals tend to be. They seem to be more worldly, somehow. I guess that makes sense, since domesticated animals have much more circumscribed lives than wild animals. When I have communicated with wild animals, they have often voiced a concern for what humans are doing to the earth. I have gone several times with groups of students to visit gray whales in Baja, Mexico. The whales always bring up the need for healing the planet and encourage us to be more like they are, in terms of social structure and cooperation. The last time we were there, the whales suggested that we work in groups to do energy healing and manifesting for the animals and the earth. I discuss how to do this in the epilogue.

TALKING WITH PLANTS AND NATURE

The earth is full of life-forms who have consciousness, spirit, and emotions; modern humans just have not had any idea that this is so. In effect, we are blind compared to indigenous people, who knew that trees, insects, and plants could talk. But finally we are rediscovering this.

Gerrie Huijts not only talks to ants but has running conversations with the plants in her garden as well. She checks in with each plant to see if it is happy. Sometimes one tells her that she forgot to water it or didn't water it enough. The plant, Gerrie says, is always right. Gerrie even talks with the seeds in her vegetable garden. Before she plants, she asks them to tell her the best time to sow.

Beth Reidel is a master gardener, herbalist, and flower essence practitioner.[1] She talks with all the plants she grows for herbs and informs them of what she is doing and why. She asks for permission before she picks any part of them. When she is attracted to a new flower to make an essence, she first sits with the flower and talks about what that particular flower's essence will be useful for. When she talks to the plants, she receives words, phrases, feelings, and pictures, just like talking with an animal.

Beth harvests some herbs from the wild, and because things are changing so much for animals and plants right now, she feels that it is essential to find out from the plants whether it is a good time and place to harvest. If there have been major habitat changes, the wild animals may need the plants more than Beth does, or it may be so dry that a particular plant won't be able to regrow well if its leaves are picked. One time, an herb told Beth not to pick it, but suggested instead that she continue hiking. Over the next hill, she found a much larger and lusher patch of the same herb that she was able to harvest. Beth believes that all beings are capable of communicating, and that the more we want that to happen, the more it will.

I spoke with a reader, Steve Stringham,[2] about his experience working with the Blackfeet Indians. He said he once asked a Blackfeet medicine man how he had discovered the medicinal uses of the plants that the Blackfeet use for healing — had he used trial and error to see which ones worked? The medicine man was shocked and told Steve that to do that would be a good way to get oneself killed. He said that the information about the plants came from the spirits who explained what each plant could do.

In my experience, you can communicate with anything that is alive. Trees are included, and the water in a stream, and so too the piece of the earth you are standing or sitting upon. All beings have consciousness and feelings: they are all alive and aware, and they are all our relatives.

COMMUNICATING WITH ALL BEINGS

EXERCISE
Out and About

When walking out in nature, be aware of any animals or plants that catch your attention. Mentally say hello to them and ask if they have a message for you. Record any impressions that pop into your head. Assume they are coming from whomever you are communicating with.

EXERCISE
Dialogues in Your Backyard

You can do this exercise with anything you find in your backyard that you would like to talk with. Get your notebook and find a comfortable place to sit. Introduce yourself and start talking. Say a few things and then stop and listen. Record whatever you think is coming back in response; whether you think it's correct or not, just write it down. Say something else, then stop and listen, and record your impressions. When you feel the conversation is finished, say thank you.

EXERCISE
Talking with Trees

Choose a tree to talk with, either one that is in your yard now or a tree you remember from your past. If you are with the tree in person, go sit with your back against it or touch it, and close your eyes. If this is a tree from your past, imagine doing this. Now introduce yourself, have your notebook ready, and ask the questions below. After each question, take a moment to be aware of whatever impressions are coming to you as a response, and record them. Then go to the next question. When you are finished, say thanks.

- Is it okay to talk with you?
- How old are you?
- Are you male or female?
- Do you have a name?
- Why did I choose you to talk with?
- What is our connection?
- Do you have any advice for me?
- Do you have any advice for humans?
- Is there anything I can do for you?

EXERCISE
Mutual Agreement

If there is an insect or wild animal, or even some garden weed, that is bothering you at your house, try this experiment in intuitive communication:

Talk with the offending animal or plant. Explain why you are bothered, what you would like to have happen, and what you are prepared to do in exchange for compliance. Make sure to keep any agreement you make. Be respectful. Explain what you will do if you don't get an agreement. Now listen to what the animal or plant has to say in response, record any impressions coming in, and assume they are coming directly from the animal or the plant. Respond and listen again for as long as you like, recording the responses. When you are finished say thanks and see what happens.

EPILOGUE
The Shift in Our World

*W*hen people learn intuitive communication with other species, they go through a door through which they can never return. Their consciousness is changed forever. I have considered cautioning my readers and students that learning intuitive communication with animals and nature may radically change their lives. Many of them switched careers, divorced from spouses who didn't support them, and decided to dedicate their lives to the animals and the earth. That's what I love about this field, and why I have stuck with it: it wakes people up and gets them paying attention to the earth.

This kind of consciousness change is needed right now on this planet because we are in such big trouble. The good news is that, although it has taken a while, most people are now becoming aware of the seriousness of the threat to life on earth, which is well portrayed in the film *The 11th Hour*, narrated by Leonardo DiCaprio. With the awareness that something is terribly wrong comes the question: "What do we do about it? How can we save the animals we hold so dear, the wild places we love, and all the joys and pleasures of being on this earth?"

I think the answer has three parts. First, get educated. It is essential to understand how we got into the mess we are in order to get out of it. Second, get active. People in every country must participate in making the change we want to experience. This might mean getting involved in politics or joining a group that is working to save the animals and the earth. People just need to get active, supporting efforts like solar power, biointensive organic gardening, local control, and sustainable lifestyles.

Third, start manifesting for a better world. The same experiments in physics that prove that we can connect intuitively simply by thinking also prove that thoughts can affect matter. The observer effect occurs not just with quantum particles, but also in the world of everyday things. What this means is that we can effect changes in the world by using the power of our thoughts and intentions.

In the Resources section (page 187) I've included resources for education, action, and manifesting to help protect the earth.

MANIFESTING FOR A BETTER WORLD

Here is a quick guide on how to manifest on an individual level and in groups.

EXERCISE
Manifesting Individually

Decide on some result or condition you want to create in your life. Form an intention statement that describes this condition as if it were already happening. For example, if you want to be doing the work you love, your statement could be: "I am now getting involved in work that I love, that fulfills my purpose in life."

Close your eyes and imagine how it would look and feel if this were true for you. Let yourself daydream, in great detail, the best possible scenario for a job, and imagine how wonderful that would be. Your statement, visualizations, and feelings are going into action in the invisible world of energy to bring about exactly what you have asked for and imagined.

Maintain this vision by doing the following:

- Restate, reimagine, and reexperience this intention daily. Do this as a short daydream session where you treat yourself to a pleasant vision of what the future could be for you.
- If you find yourself thinking negatively, say, "Cancel that." Replace the negative thought with a positive one that cancels it out.
- Call on any higher power, angels, spirits, or guides you like to help you manifest.
- Do something new each week that helps bring your vision into reality.

EXERCISE
Manifesting in a Group

- Each person decides on something he or she wants to manifest for the world.
- Each person takes a turn stating an intention out loud for the group, describing the vision behind the intention as if it were already in the process of happening. Be specific. For example, a vision statement for the world could be: all governments in the world are becoming more humanitarian and are working together to reverse global warming and create a sustainable world.
- As the person describes the vision, everyone in the group, with eyes closed, imagines and experiences that vision vividly, in as much detail as possible, as if it were already in the process of happening.

- Everyone sends a feeling of love and hope to that vision.
- Keep going until each person in the group has had a chance to state an intention and describe a vision.
- Before you end the group, discuss practical actions you can take to support those visions coming into reality. Commit to taking at least one action per vision.
- Each time you meet, review the items you worked on and note any results from the real world.

You can work on the personal and planetary level concurrently; both are needed. We cannot help the planet if we are not well — emotionally, physically, and spiritually — so it is important to always manifest for your own good and your own happiness. Try these techniques on your own and with your friends.

SAVING CHARLIE

To show you how manifesting can work, here is an example of a successful manifesting project.

When I was with a group of students visiting whales in Baja, Mexico, we encountered a very ill dog who was hanging out at the dock where we launched our kayaks. When we boated back from the island where we camped on Magdalena Bay, the dog was still there, still stray, and still pink all over from a skin condition, looking miserable. We wanted to take him with us, but the driver of

our van thought the dog was contagious to people and did not want him in his vehicle. The dog was all alone, and we all knew he would not last long. Before we left, Julie Hendrickson from our group asked the fishermen in the area to feed him, but we left feeling depressed about the whole thing.

Charlie in Baja

After about twenty minutes of driving en route to the Sea of Cortez, we hatched a plot for rescuing the dog, who had told Julie he wanted to be called Charlie. By the time we arrived at the Sea of Cortez, the plan was gaining momentum. We would ask the kayak guides back at the whale camp to talk to the boat captains in the area and find someone who would be willing to drive the dog across the peninsula. The next day, Julie started making calls. The rest of us went out to watch

Cheryl and Charlie

whales and birds, visit a tidal hot spring, and snorkel, but we kept Charlie in our minds and imagined everything going smoothly in his rescue.

While we were away, two boat captains from Magdalena Bay agreed to go to the launch site, find Charlie, and bring him to us. When Charlie arrived that evening, we examined him, and it turned out he had mange, was covered in fleas, and was severely sunburned. Now we began manifesting to find a place where he could be kept until he was well enough to travel to the United States. The next day Julie took him into town to a veterinary clinic and gave him a good bath. There she found out about a local pet rescue group that was willing to treat Charlie and care for him until Julie could have him flown to the United States.

We left Mexico knowing that Charlie would be okay. But Julie still had to find a home for him, as she already had her limit of dogs. The owner of Blue Waters, the tour company that hosted our trip in Baja, volunteered to drive Charlie up to California and ended up finding Charlie a home through his friends. About six months later, Charlie and his new owner showed up at a class I taught in Santa Rosa, California. I've included a picture of Charlie with his new mom, Cheryl Best, in his new life.

I tell all my students that all they have to do to be able to talk intuitively to animals and nature is to believe it is possible and then start practicing. Well, it is also possible for us to shift our world and make it be the way we want it to be. We just have to believe that it is possible and start making it happen.

Notes

INTRODUCTION

1. Adele Leas practices and teaches Jin Shin Jyutsu with animals, and she has published a book about it, *Jin Shin Jyutsu for Your Companion Animal* (for details, see www.jsjforyouranimal.com).

CHAPTER 1: ABOUT INTUITIVE COMMUNICATION

1. Danny K. Alford, "The Origin of Speech in a Deep Structure of Psi," *Phoenix: New Directions in the Study of Man* 2, no. 2 (Fall/Winter 1978); and "Not Just Words," *Redux, the Newsletter of Language and Consciousness* 1, no. 1 (March 2002): 8. Both are available at www.enformy.com.

   Alford, also known as Moonhawk, died an untimely death in 2002 from cancer. At the time, he was earning a PhD in linguistics at the University of California at Berkeley, and he had studied physics. Part Native American, he had spent time with the Northern Cheyenne and Navajo, learning both languages and eventually teaching Navajo on the reservation. A friend of Moonhawk's posted his work at www.enformy.com. Besides the articles above, his work is unpublished (as far as I know), but you can download it from the website if you're interested.

2. The research and experiments by Walter Greist come from an unpublished graduate paper he sent to me: "Psispeech Communication," May 22, 1976. Greist is now an organic farmer and no longer working in the field of psi research, but he still retains a keen interest.

In the paper, Greist described his psi experiments. In one experiment, he played a tape of himself recounting an adventure he'd experienced to two groups of people. With the first group, he stopped the tape before the story ended, then he gave the people in the group a choice of five possible endings to the story and asked them to guess what actually happened. He did the same thing with the second group, but Greist stayed in the room with them throughout, and when the group had to guess the end of the story, Greist mentally sent them information about the actual ending. The people in the second group still had to guess, but they had the benefit of Greist's directed thoughts in making that guess. Greist repeated the experiment with a number of stories. The results showed that the people in the second group (who received the researcher's directed mental thoughts) were significantly more accurate in choosing the correct ending to the story than the first group. In his experiments, Greist found that neither speech nor psi was as strong alone as when they were used together.

3. Ronald Rose, *Primitive Psychic Power* (Toronto: Signet Mystic Books, 1968).

4. McTaggart's book *The Field* is an examination of new theories in physics. Lynne McTaggart, *The Field: The Quest for the Secret Force of the Universe* (New York: HarperCollins, 2001). However, most of the information here is from Lynne McTaggart, *The Intention Experiment: Using Your Thoughts to Change Your Life and Your World* (New York: Free Press/Simon & Schuster, 2007).

5. McTaggart, *The Intention Experiment*, 13.
6. The stories about Cleave Baxter here are taken from McTaggart, *The Intention Experiment*, 35–46. Backster also wrote a book about his findings: Cleave Backster, *Primary Perception: Biocommunication in Plants, Living Foods and Human Cells* (Anza, CA: White Rose Millenium Press, 2003).
7. Baxter later learned that waxy buildup between cells in plants causes the kind of discharge he saw that day.
8. The information about Fritz Popp and Konstantin Korotkov is from McTaggart, *The Intention Experiment*, 41–46.
9. Rupert Sheldrake, *Dogs That Know When Their Owners Are Coming Home and Other Unexplained Powers of Animals* (New York: Crown Publishers, 1999).

CHAPTER 2: TO HEAR AND BE HEARD

1. Some animal communicators say that animals are only able to perceive information intuitively in pictures, and they advise people to send information to animals only in pictures. I believe this is another example of humans deciding that animals aren't as adept at something as we are. In my experience, animals are quite capable of perceiving thoughts, words, and feelings intuitively.
2. Carolyn Resnick has written a book titled *Naked Liberty: Memoirs of My Childhood* (Lubbock, TX: Amigo Publications, 2005).
3. Bekoff, Marc, *The Emotional Lives of Animals: A Leading Scientist Explores Animal Joy, Sorrow, and Empathy and Why They Matter* (Novato, CA: New World Library, 2007).

CHAPTER 3: PACK OF TWO

1. Caroline Knapp, *Pack of Two: The Intricate Bond between People and Dogs* (New York: Dell Publishing, 1998).
2. Suzanne Clothier, *Bones Would Rain from the Sky: Deepening*

Our Relationships with Dogs (New York: Time Warner Book Group, 2002), 29.

CHAPTER 4: CREATING THE PEACEABLE KINGDOM

1. Clicker training uses a click noise to signal to an animal when a behavior is approved of. The click is coupled with a treat. Clicker training is an effective nonviolent training method.

CHAPTER 5: ADDING INTUITION TO ANIMAL TRAINING

1. The barefoot trim is relatively new to the horse world. Most farriers still trim to leave a high heel and a short toe and many cut into the sole of the foot when trimming. I can personally attest that these practices lead to lameness in horses. For more information on barefoot trimming, see the Resources section, page 182.

2. Emma Parsons, *Click to Calm: Healing the Aggressive Dog* (Waltham, MA: Sunshine Books, 2004). For more on clicker training, see the Resources section, page 183.

3. Mark Rashid, *Life Lessons from a Ranch Horse* (Boulder, CO: Johnson Books, 2003).

4. Jan Fennell, *The Dog Listener: Learn How to Communicate with Your Dog for Willing Cooperation* (New York: Harper-Collins Publishers, 2004).

CHAPTER 6: DEALING WITH BAD BEHAVIORS

1. Positive-reinforcement animal training programs involve the use of treats, praise, and/or play as a reward for good behavior. Negative training techniques, such as yelling, hitting, or other violent methods, are avoided. For more, see the Resources section, page 183.

2. One of the veterinarians I have worked with told me that kidney function can be tested by doing a specific gravity test on the urine, which is less expensive than running a blood panel for the kidney. Such a test measures the specific gravity of urine compared to that of water. If your animal's values deviate from the norm, it indicates a problem with kidney functioning.

CHAPTER 7: AIDING AN ANIMAL IN DISTRESS

1. Energy healing involves working with invisible fields of energy in the body to balance the body and promote health. There are many methods of energy healing, but the basic premise of all of them is that pain, disease, and any physical problem stem from an energy block or imbalance in the body.
2. The website for Give a Dog a Bone is www.gadab.org. The foundation helps foster animals caught in the legal system.
3. These mares were used to make Premarin, a drug prescribed for menopausal women. Mares are kept in tight stalls and kept constantly pregnant so that the hormones in their urine can be collected. The mares are discarded to the auction pens after a few years of "service" and all their babies are sent for slaughter. Aside from being incredibly cruel and therefore not something you would want to support, the drug has now been found to have dangerous side effects.

CHAPTER 9: COPING WITH DEATH

1. When a horse is insulin-resistant, it means the horse can't handle anything high in sugar, such as unlimited grazing on fresh grass, alfalfa hay, oats, cookies, apples, carrots, molasses, and candy. Laminitis is an inflammation of the hoof that can be caused by insulin-resistance, and it can lead to crippling lameness.

CHAPTER 10: INTUITIVE VOICE IN
THE WILDERNESS

1. Flower essences are made by picking a flower and placing it in water for a period of time. The water is then said to take on the essence of the flower. See the Resources section, page 186, for more information.

2. Steve Stringham runs a program for viewing bears in Alaska, and he has written several books on bears. His website is www.bear-viewing-in-alaska.info.

Resources

*T*his section focuses on holistic care and training of dogs, cats, and horses but also includes resources for finding lost animals, getting better informed about what is going on in the world, and getting involved in helping save the earth. These resources are a sampling of the best I have come across in my research, but the list is not definitive or comprehensive. Keeping abreast of the best, most current resources is a never-ending process. Whenever you search for a solution to a problem with your animal, check out all your options. Ask your friends what they have done and who they know, and search the Internet to discover the most current information available for your issue.

HOLISTIC DIET AND CARE

To find a holistic veterinarian in the United States, visit the website of the American Holistic Veterinary Medical Association: www.holisticvetlist.com.

Dogs and Cats

Books

Arora, Sandy. *Whole Health for Happy Cats: A Guide to Keeping Your Cat Naturally Healthy, Happy, and Well-Fed.* Dallas, TX: Quarry Books, 2006.

Billinghurst, Ian. *The Barf Diet: Raw Feeding for Dogs and Cats Using Evolutionary Principles.* Lithgow, Australia: self-published, 2003.

Flaim, Denise, and Michael W. Fox. *The Holistic Dog Book: Canine Care for the 21st Century.* Indianapolis, IN: Howell Book House, 2003.

Frazier, Anitra. *The New Natural Cat: A Complete Guide for Finicky Owners.* New York: Plume, 1990.

Goldstein, Martin. *The Nature of Animal Healing: The Definitive Holistic Medicine Guide to Caring for Your Dog and Cat.* New York: Ballantine Books, 2000.

Pitcairn, Richard H., and Susan Hubble Pitcairn. *Dr. Pitcairn's New Complete Guide to Natural Health for Dogs and Cats.* New York: Rodale Books, 2005. This guide includes diet information.

Websites

Feline Instincts, www.felineinstincts.com: For a complete diet for cats and dogs, just add fresh, organic, raw meat to their mix.

Only Natural Pet Store, www.onlynaturalpet.com: Offers the Natural Flea Care system and holistic supplements and products.

Horses

Books

Jackson, Jaime. *Paddock Paradise: A Guide to Natural Horse Boarding.* Harrison, AR: Star Ridge Publishing, 2007.

Ramey, Pete. *Making Natural Hoofcare Work for You.* Harrison, AR: Star Ridge Publishing, 2003.

Websites

Hoof Rehabilitation Specialists, www.hoofrehab.com: This is Pete Ramey's website, giving in-depth information on the natural trim for horses' feet.

Safer Grass, www.safergrass.org/articles/managegrazing.html: This website provides information on how to care for horses with laminitis, and how to graze horses safely.

For supplements and herbs, see the following sites:

Dynamite, www.dynamiteonline.com: For minerals, supplements, and food.

Forco, www.forco.com/main/index.asp: Sells a probiotic for horses to aid digestion.

Herb-n-Horse, www.herbnhorse.com

Hilton Herbs, www.hiltonherbs.com

Robert McDowell's Herbal Treatments, www.herbal-treatments.com

NONVIOLENT TRAINING METHODS
Dogs

These references will help you with all your training issues and teach you how to become the leader of your dog without using violence.

Books

Cantrell, Krista. *Housetrain Your Dog Now.* New York: Plume, 2000. Focuses on house training.

Fennell, Jan. *The Dog Listener.* New York: Collins, 2004. Helpful for calming and establishing leadership and for hyper, insecure, anxious, or pushy dogs.

McConnell, Patricia. *The Cautious Canine.* Black Earth, WI: Dog's Best Friend, 2005. Helpful for aggressive dogs.

Parsons, Emma. *Click to Calm: Healing the Aggressive Dog.* A Karen Pryor Clicker Training Book. Waltham, MA: Sunshine Books, 2004. Helpful for aggressive dogs.

Rugaas, Turid. *On Talking Terms with Dogs: Calming Signals.* Wenatchee, WA: Dogwise Publishing, 2005.

Rugaas, Turid. *My Dog Pulls, What Do I Do?* Wenatchee, WA: Dogwise Publishing, 2005.

Ryan, Terry, and Kirsten Mortensen. *Outwitting Dogs: Revolutionary Techniques for Dog Training That Work.* Guilford, CT: Lyons Press, 2004.

DVD

Really Reliable Recall — Train Your Dog to Come When Called . . . No Matter What! (Healthy Dog Productions, 2007; for U.S. and Canada DVD formats only). This DVD will help with dogs who won't come when called.

Website

Clickertraining.com, www.clickertraining.com: This is Karen Pryor's website offering books and supplies for learning the clicker training method.

Cats

Books

Bennett, Pam Johnson. *Twisted Whiskers: Solving Your Cat's Behavior Problems*. New South Wales, Australia: Crossing Press, 1994.

Halls, Vicki. *How to Be a Cat Detective: Solving the Mystery of Your Cat's Behavior*. New York: Gotham, 2006.

McConnell, Patricia. *The Fastidious Feline: How to Prevent and Treat Litter Box Problems*. Madison, WI: Dog's Best Friend, 1996.

Websites

Affordable Cat Fence, www.catfence.com: This nonelectric, angled-in fence method keeps your cats in your backyard while keeping other cats out and can help deter unwanted urination.

Catscratching.com, www.catscratching.com: For help with preventing furniture scratching.

Precious Cat Litter, www.preciouscat.com: Provides advice for litter-box problems and sells a special litter that attracts cats.

Purrfect Cat Behavior Guide, www.purrfectcatbehavior.com: Covers many behavior problems.

Horses

Books

Lindley, Kathleen. *In the Company of Horses: A Year on the Road with Horseman Mark Rashid*. Boulder, CO: Johnson Books, 2006.

Rashid, Mark. *Life Lessons of a Ranch Horse*. Devon, United Kingdom: David & Charles, 2004.

Resnick, Carolyn. *Naked Liberty: Memoirs of My Childhood*. Los Olivos, CA: Amigo Publications, 2005.

Tellington-Jones, Linda, and Bobbie Lieberman. *The Ultimate Horse Behavior and Training.* Chicago: Trafalgar Square Books, 2006.

Video
Liberty Training by Carolyn Resnick: Order this horse-training video through www.dancewithhorses.com.

Websites
Barefoot Saddle, www.barefootsaddle.com: Sells treeless saddles.

The Bitless Bridle, www.bitlessbridle.com: Learn about bitless bridles on this website.

The Clicker Center, www.theclickercenter.com: Alexandra Kurland's clicker training.

Kaaren Jordan, www.kaarenjordan.com: For information on treeless saddles and bitless bridles.

Parelli, www.parelli.com: Parelli offers a popular natural horsemanship training program, including DVDs.

Mark Rashid Horse Training, www.markrashid.com: Rashid is also a natural horse trainer. Check this site for his books and DVDs.

Tellington TTouch Training, www.ttouch.com: This site has books and DVDs about Linda Tellington Jones's natural horse and dog training methods.

Torsion Saddles, www.gotreeless.com: Sells treeless saddles.

CARE AND TRAINING AIDS
Acupuncture, Acupressure, Chiropractic, and Jin Shin Jyutsu

These modalities can help with a whole range of problems. To find an acupuncturist or veterinary chiropractor in the United States, check the website of the American Holistic Veterinary Medical Association (www.holisticvetlist.com).

Books
Schwartz, Cheryl, *Four Paws Five Directions.* Berkeley, CA: Ten Speed Press and Celestial Arts, 1996.

Zidonis, Nancy. *Equine Acupressure: A Working Manual.* Larkspur, CO: Tallgrass Publishers, 1999.

Websites
Tallgrass Animal Acupressure Institute, www.animal-acupressure .com: Offers information, courses, books, and lists of practitioners.
Jin Shin Jyutsu for Your Animals, www.jsjforyouranimal.com: Offers information and Adele Leas's book.

Flower Essences

Flower essences are made in such a way as to capture the essence of a flower and are used to address subtle and emotional issues in the body. There are many flower essence resources. Here are a few I like to use:

Flower Essence Society, www.flowersociety.org: For information on American and English flower essences.
The Unified Field, www.theunifiedfield.com: From this website, you can order Australian flower essences and Dutch blossom remedies.

Homeopathy

Homeopathy is a method of healing that uses minute quantities of substances to trigger the body's own healing tendencies. There are many more books on homeopathy in addition to those listed below.

Books
Hamilton, Don. *Homeopathic Care for Cats and Dogs: Small Doses for Small Animals.* Berkeley, CA: North Atlantic Books, 1999.
Shaw, Susan, *Homeopathy for Horses: A Layperson's Guide.* Nelson, BC: The Original Farmhouse, 2005.

Website
Tallgrass Animal Acupressure Institute, www.animalacupressure .com: They also offer books on homeopathy.

Massage

There are many different styles of massage for animals. To find a trained animal body worker, ask your friends and your veterinarian, and ask at the local pet food store and feed store. Here are a few massage resources that show you how to do it yourself.

Books
Ballner, Maryjean. *Cat Massage: A Whiskers-to-Tail Guide to Your Cat's Ultimate Petting Experience.* New York: St. Martin's Griffin, 1997.
Blingnault, Karen. *Stretching Exercises for Your Horse: The Path to Perfect Suppleness.* Chicago: Trafalgar Square Books, 2003.
Fox, Michael. *The Healing Touch for Dogs: The Proven Massage Program for Dogs.* New York: Newmarket Press, 2004.

Website
Tellington TTouch Training, www.ttouch.com: Linda Tellington Jones's unique form of bodywork called TTouch.

LOST ANIMAL RESOURCES

For information on how to search for a lost animal, check the Pet Rescue website (www.petrescue.com).

To hire a search dog to track your lost animal, check with Missing Pet Partnership (www.missingpetpartnership.org), to see if there is a trained missing-pet search-and-rescue dog in your area.

PROTECTING THE EARTH

These are thousands of ways to get more informed and more involved in protecting the earth. Here are just a handful.

Alternative Sources of Information about What Is Happening in the World

Architects and Engineers for 9/11 Truth, www.ae911truth.org: A new look at the 9/11 tragedy.
Air America Radio, www.airamerica.com

Centre for Research on Globalization, www.globalresearch.ca
Go Left TV, www.goleft.tv
Pacifica National Radio, www.pacifica.org
The 11th Hour, www.11thhouraction.com: Action groups centered around the movie.
The Corporation, www.thecorporation.com: News and organizations inspired by the film.
An Inconvenient Truth, www.climatecrisis.net: News and action inspired by the film.

Organizations Dedicated to Saving the Planet

Greenpeace, www.greenpeace.org/international
Natural Resources Defense Council, www.nrdc.org

Living Sustainably on the Earth

Websites
Sustainable Communities Network, www.sustainable.org: Offers books, information, and other ways to get involved.
Wiser Earth, www.wiserearth.org: World index of social and environmental responsibility.

Book
Hawkins, Paul. *Blessed Unrest: How the Largest Movement in the World Came into Being and Why No One Saw it Coming.* New York: Viking, 2007.

MANIFESTING A BETTER FUTURE FOR OURSELVES AND THE WORLD

Books
Losier, Michael. *The Law of Attraction.* Victoria, BC: Michael J. Losier Enterprises, 2006.
McColl, Peggy. *Your Destiny Switch.* Carlsbad, CA: Hay House, 2007.
McTaggart, Lynne. *The Intention Experiment: Using Your Thoughts to Change Your Life and the World.* New York: Free Press, 2007.

Recommended Reading

INTUITIVE ABILITY, COMMUNICATION, AND CONNECTION

Bohm, David. *The Undivided Universe*. New York: Routledge, 1995.

Boone, J. Allen. *Kinship with All Life*. New York: Harper & Brothers, 1954.

———. *Adventures in Kinship with All Life*. Joshua Tree, CA: Tree of Life Publications, 1990.

Choquette, Sonia. *The Psychic Pathway: A Workbook for Reawakening the Voice of Your Soul*. New York: Crown Trade Paperbacks, 1995.

———. *Trust Your Vibes: Secret Tools for Six-Sensory Living*. Carlsbad, CA: Hay House, 2005.

———. *Trust Your Vibes at Work and Let Them Work for You!* Carlsbad, CA: Hay House, 2006.

Dunbar, Ian. *Before and After Getting Your Puppy: The Positive Approach to Raising a Happy, Healthy, and Well-Behaved Dog*. Novato, CA: New World Library, 2004.

Getten, Mary. *Communicating with Orcas, the Whales' Perspective*. Victoria, BC: Trafford Publishing, 2006.

Graff, Dale. *Tracks in the Psychic Wilderness: An Exploration of*

Remote Viewing, ESP, Precognitive Dreaming and Synchronicity. Boston: Element Books, 1998.

Gurney, Carol. *The Language of Animals: 7 Steps to Communicating with Animals*. New York: Dell Publishing, 2001.

Kinkade, Amelia. *Straight from the Horse's Mouth: How to Talk to Animals and Get Answers*. Novato, CA: New World Library, 2001.

———. *The Language of Miracles: A Celebrated Psychic Teaches You to Talk to Animals*. Novato, CA: New World Library, 2006.

Lasher, Margot. *And the Animals Will Teach You: Discovering Ourselves through Our Relationships with Animals*. New York: Berkeley Books, 1996.

Lauck, Joanne Elizabeth. *The Voice of the Infinite in the Small: Revisioning the Insect-Human Connection*. Boston: Shambhala, 2002.

MacKay, Nicci. *Spoken in Whispers: The Autobiography of a Horse Whisperer*. New York: Fireside, 1997.

Masson, Jeffrey, and Susan McCarthy. *When Elephants Weep: The Emotional Lives of Animals*. New York: Bantam Doubleday Dell Publishing Group, 1995.

McElroy, Susan Chernak. *Animals as Teachers and Healers: True Stories and Reflections*. Troutdale, OR: New Sage Press, 1996.

Myers, Arthur. *Communicating with Animals: The Spiritual Connection Between People and Animals*. Chicago: Contemporary Books, 1997.

Naparstek, Belleruth. *Your Sixth Sense: Activating Your Psychic Potential*. New York: HarperCollins, 1997.

Ostrander, Sheila, and Lynn Schroeder. *Psychic Discoveries Behind the Iron Curtain*. Englewood Cliffs, NJ: Prentice Hall, 1970.

———. *The ESP Papers: Scientists Speak Out from Behind the Iron Curtain*. New York: Bantam Books, 1996.

Puthoff, Charles, and Russell Targ. *The Mind Race: Understanding and Using Psychic Ability*. New York: Random House, 1984.

Radkin, Dean. *The Conscious Universe: The Scientific Truth of Psychic Phenomena*. New York: HarperCollins, 1997.

Rose, Ronald. *Primitive Psychic Power*. Toronto: Signet Mystic Books, 1968.

Russell, Peter. *The Global Brain Awakens: Our Next Evolutionary Leap*. Palo Alto, CA: Global Brain, 1995.

Sanders, Pete, Jr. *You Are Psychic*. New York: Fawcett Columbine Books, 1989.

Schultz, Mona Lisa. *Awakening Intuition: Using Your Mind-Body Network for Insight and Healing*. New York: Harmony Books, 1998.

Schwartz, Gary. *The Living Energy Universe*. Charlottesville, VA: Hampton Roads Publishing Company, 1999.

———. *The Afterlife Experiments: Breakthrough Scientific Evidence of Life after Death*. New York: Pocket Books, 2002.

Seed, John, and Joanna Macy. *Thinking Like a Mountain: Toward a Council of All Beings*. Gabriola Island, BC: New Society Publishers, 1988.

Sheldrake, Rupert. *Dogs That Know When Their Owners Are Coming Home and Other Unexplained Powers of Animals*. New York: Crown Publishers, 1999.

Targ, Russell. *Limitless Mind: A Guide to Remote Viewing and Transformation of Consciousness*. Novato, CA: New World Library, 2004.

Targ, Russell, and Jane Katra. *Miracles of the Mind: Exploring Nonlocal Consciousness and Spiritual Healing*. Novato, CA: New World Library, 1999.

NATURE

Andrews, Ted. *Animal Speak: The Spiritual and Magical Powers of Creatures Great and Small*. Woodbury, MN: Llewellyn, 1996.

———. *Nature Speak: Signs, Omens & Messages in Nature*. Jackson, TN: Dragonhawk Publishers, 2004.

Bekoff, Marc. *The Emotional Lives of Animals: A Leading Scientist Explores Animal Joy, Sorrow, and Empathy — and Why They Matter*. Novato, CA: New World Library, 2007.

Grauds, Connie. *Jungle Medicine*. San Rafael, CA: Center for Spirited Medicine, 2004.

Hogan, Linda, and Brenda Peterson. *The Sweet Breathing of Plants: Women Writing on the Green World*. New York: North Point Press, 2001.

Johnson, Buffie. *Lady of the Beasts: The Goddess and Her Sacred Animals*. Rochester, VT: Inner Traditions International, 1994.

Louv, Richard. *Last Child in the Woods: Saving Our Children from Nature Deficit Disorder*. Chapel Hill, NC: Algonquin Books, 2005.

Macy, Joanna. *World as Lover, World as Self*. Berkeley, CA: Parallax Press, 1991.

Sams, Jamie, and David Carson. *Medicine Cards: The Discovery of Power Through the Ways of Animals*. New York: St. Martin's Press, 1988.

Seed, John, and Joanna Macy. *Thinking Like a Mountain: Toward a Council of All Beings*. Gabriola Island, BC: New Society Publishers, 1988.

Skafte, Dianne. *When Oracles Speak — Understanding the Signs and Symbols All Around Us*. Wheaton, IL: Quest Books, 2000.

Tompkins, Peter, and Christopher Bird. *The Secret Life of Plants*. New York: Harper & Row Publishers, 1973.

MEDICAL INTUITION AND ENERGY HEALING

Coates, Margit. *Healing for Horses: The Essential Guide to Using Hands-On Healing Energy with Horses*. New York: Sterling Publishers, 2002.

Eden, Donna. *Energy Medicine*. New York: Tarcher, 1999.

———. *The Energy Medicine Kit*. Louisville, CO: Sounds True, 2005.

Motz, Julie. *Hands of Life*. New York: Bantam Books, 1998.

Schultz, Mona Lisa. *Awakening Intuition: Using Your Mind-Body Network for Insight and Healing*. New York: Harmony Books, 1998.

Stein, Diane. *Essential Reiki: A Complete Guide to an Ancient Healing Art*. New South Wales, Australia: Crossing Press, 1998.

Wilde, Clare. *Hands-On Energy Therapy for Horses and Riders*. North Pomfret, VT: Trafalgar Square Publishing, 1999.

ROOTS OF THE ECOLOGICAL CRISIS

Eisler, Riane. *The Chalice and the Blade: Our History, Our Future*. San Francisco: Harper San Francisco, 1988.

————. *The Power of Partnership: The Seven Relationships That Will Change Your Life*. Novato, CA: New World Library, 2002.

Gimbutas, Marija. *The Civilization of the Goddess*. New York: Thames & Hudson, 2001.

Jensen, Derrick. *A Language Older Than Words*. New York: Context Books, 2000.

Johnson, Buffie. *Lady of the Beasts: The Goddess and Her Sacred Animals*. Rochester, VT: Inner Traditions International, 1994.

Lash, John Lamb. *Not in His Image: Gnostic Vision, Sacred Ecology, and the Future of Belief*. White River Junction, VT: Chelsea Green, 2006.

Macy, Joanna. *Coming Back to Life: Practices to Reconnect Our Lives, Our World*. Gabriola Island, BC: New Society Publishers, 1998.

Marler, Joan, ed. *From the Realm of the Ancestors*. Manchester, CT: Knowledge, Ideas and Trends, 1997.

Singer, Peter. *Animal Liberation*. New York: Ecco Press, 2001.

Sjoo, Monica. *Return of the Dark Light Mother or New Age Armageddon?* Austin, TX: Plain View Press, 1999.

Stone, Christopher. *Should Trees Have Standing? And Other Essays on Laws, Morals and the Environment*. Dobbs Ferry, NY: Oceana Publications, 1996.

Index

About the Author

*M*arta Williams holds an undergraduate degree in natural resource conservation from the University of California at Berkeley and a master's degree in biology from San Francisco State University. Before becoming an animal communicator, she worked for many years as a wildlife biologist and environmental scientist.

The author of *Beyond Words* and *Learning Their Language*, Marta provides intuitive consultations for all types of animals, working with clients throughout the world by phone and email. She lives in Northern California and travels internationally to lecture and teach workshops on intuitive communication with animals and nature. To schedule a consultation or to find out about attending or hosting a workshop, visit her website at www.martawilliams.com.

NEW WORLD LIBRARY is dedicated to publishing books and other media that inspire and challenge us to improve the quality of our lives and the world.

We are a socially and environmentally aware company, and we strive to embody the ideals presented in our publications. We recognize that we have an ethical responsibility to our customers, our staff members, and our planet.

We serve our customers by creating the finest publications possible on personal growth, creativity, spirituality, wellness, and other areas of emerging importance. We serve New World Library employees with generous benefits, significant profit sharing, and constant encouragement to pursue their most expansive dreams.

As a member of the Green Press Initiative, we print an increasing number of books with soy-based ink on 100 percent postconsumer-waste recycled paper. Also, we power our offices with solar energy and contribute to nonprofit organizations working to make the world a better place for us all.

Our products are available
in bookstores everywhere.
For our catalog, please contact:

New World Library
14 Pamaron Way
Novato, California 94949

Phone: 415-884-2100 or 800-972-6657
Catalog requests: Ext. 50
Orders: Ext. 52
Fax: 415-884-2199
Email: escort@newworldlibrary.com

To subscribe to our electronic newsletter, visit
www.newworldlibrary.com